Education Reform in Mozambique

# Education Reform in Mozambique

*Lessons and Challenges*

Louise Fox, Lucrecia Santibañez, Vy Nguyen, and Pierre André

**THE WORLD BANK**
Washington, D.C.

© 2012 International Bank for Reconstruction and Development / International Development Association or The World Bank
1818 H Street NW
Washington DC 20433
Telephone: 202-473-1000
Internet: www.worldbank.org

1 2 3 4   15 14 13 12

This volume is a product of the staff of The World Bank with external contributions. The findings, interpretations, and conclusions expressed in this volume do not necessarily reflect the views of The World Bank, its Board of Executive Directors, or the governments they represent.

The World Bank does not guarantee the accuracy of the data included in this work. The boundaries, colors, denominations, and other information shown on any map in this work do not imply any judgment on the part of The World Bank concerning the legal status of any territory or the endorsement or acceptance of such boundaries.

**Rights and Permissions**
The material in this work is subject to copyright. Because The World Bank encourages dissemination of its knowledge, this work may be reproduced, in whole or in part, for noncommercial purposes as long as full attribution to the work is given.

For permission to reproduce any part of this work for commercial purposes, please send a request with complete information to the Copyright Clearance Center Inc., 222 Rosewood Drive, Danvers, MA 01923, USA; telephone: 978-750-8400; fax: 978-750-4470; Internet: www.copyright.com.

All other queries on rights and licenses, including subsidiary rights, should be addressed to the Office of the Publisher, The World Bank, 1818 H Street NW, Washington, DC 20433, USA; fax: 202-522-2422; e-mail: pubrights@worldbank.org.

ISBN (paper): 978-0-8213-8975-1
ISBN (electronic): 978-0-8213-8976-8
DOI: 10.1596/978-0-8213-8975-1

**Library of Congress Cataloging-in-Publication Data**
Education reform in Mozambique : lessons and challenges / Louise Fox ... [et al.].
   p. cm.
   Includes bibliographical references.
   ISBN 978-0-8213-8975-1 — ISBN 978-0-8213-8976-8 (electronic)
   1. Education—Mozambique—Longitudinal studies. 2. Educational change—Mozambique. I. Fox, M. Louise.
   LA1986.E38 2012+
   370.968—dc23

2011051986

*Cover photo:* Child writing on the board, Primary School of Nhanpfuine. © Eric Miller/The World Bank.
*Cover design:* Naylor Design, Inc.

# Contents

*Acknowledgments*   *xi*
*About the Authors*   *xiii*
*Abbreviations*   *xv*

| | | |
|---|---|---|
| **Chapter 1** | **Introduction** | 1 |
| | The Education Challenge | 2 |
| | Organization of This Report | 6 |
| | Notes | 7 |
| | References | 7 |
| **Chapter 2** | **Conceptual Framework and Data** | 9 |
| | Education Supply and Demand | 10 |
| | Data and Sources | 12 |
| | References | 14 |
| **Chapter 3** | **Analysis of the Effects of the 2004–05 Reforms:** | |
| | **Outputs and Outcomes** | 15 |
| | Primary Education | 15 |
| | Costs Affect Access | 18 |
| | 2004 Reforms | 20 |
| | Effects of Late Entry, Long Completion Times | 21 |

|  |  |  |
|---|---|---|
|  | Vulnerable Groups: Orphans | 24 |
|  | Completion Rates | 27 |
|  | Secondary Education | 32 |
|  | Private Sector Education Is Growing | 36 |
|  | Quality at Issue | 37 |
|  | Notes | 39 |
|  | References | 40 |
| **Chapter 4** | **The Effects of the Primary Reforms: Econometric Analysis** | **41** |
|  | References | 44 |
| **Chapter 5** | **Does Education Matter for Poverty Reduction? A Livelihoods Perspective** | **45** |
|  | Household Enterprises and Poverty Reduction | 47 |
|  | Education Needs of the Labor Force | 48 |
|  | Notes | 51 |
|  | References | 51 |
| **Chapter 6** | **Investing in Education: Tough Choices Ahead** | **53** |
|  | Policy Tradeoffs and the General Question of Access | 54 |
|  | Emphasize Primary or Secondary? | 58 |
|  | Policy Options for Mozambique | 59 |
|  | Education in Mozambique: A Bright Future | 68 |
|  | Notes | 70 |
|  | References | 71 |
| **Appendixes** |  | **73** |
| **Appendix A** | **Additional Tables from the Analysis** | **75** |
|  | Primary Education: Enrollment Rates and Factors Affecting Enrollment | 75 |
|  | Secondary Education: Enrollment Rates and School Expenditures | 82 |
| **Appendix B** | **Simulation of Enrollment Rate Scenarios** | **89** |
|  | Main Simulation | 89 |
|  | Standard Errors | 90 |
|  | Simulation with Double Transition Rates | 90 |

| Appendix C | Econometric Estimation of the Program Effect | 93 |
|---|---|---|
| | The Basic Model: Effect of the Program for the Exposed Group | 93 |
| | The Extended Model: Effect of the Program for Each Age | 97 |
| | Other Determinants of Enrollment | 101 |
| | Notes | 101 |
| | References | 101 |

**Boxes**

| 1.1 | Mozambique At a Glance | 2 |
|---|---|---|
| 1.2 | Map of Provinces in Mozambique | 3 |
| 1.3 | Education System in Mozambique | 4 |
| 2.1 | The "Malleable" Nature of Education Supply | 11 |
| 2.2 | Description of Survey Data Used in the Analysis | 13 |
| 4.1 | Difficulties of Assessing Reform Impact | 42 |
| 5.1 | Household Enterprises | 47 |
| 6.1 | Two Common Tradeoffs in Education Policy | 60 |
| 6.2 | Would Early Childhood Development (ECD) Programs in Mozambique Get Children to Start School on Time? | 62 |
| 6.3 | Conditional Cash Transfers in Mozambique: A Simulation Exercise | 64 |
| 6.4 | "Rules of Thumb" Financial Training Can Improve Business Management for Household and Micro Entrepreneurs | 69 |

**Figures**

| 3.1 | Gross Enrollment Rates in Primary Schools, 1997, 2003, 2008 | 16 |
|---|---|---|
| 3.2 | Age-Relevant Enrollment Rate by Consumption Quintile, 2008 | 17 |
| 3.3 | Comparison of Annual Per Student Expenditures on Obligatory Contributions (fees) in EP1, 2003 and 2008 (constant 2008 prices) | 19 |
| 3.4 | Comparison of Annual Per Student Expenditures on Obligatory Contributions (fees) in EP2, 2003 and 2008 (constant 2008 prices) | 20 |
| 3.5 | Net Enrollment Rates in Primary Schools, 1997, 2003, 2008 | 22 |
| 3.6 | Children Attending EP1 and EP2 Schools by Age, 2003 and 2008 | 23 |

| | | |
|---|---|---|
| 3.7 | Children Not Attending School, by Age, 2003 and 2008 | 26 |
| 3.8 | Dropout Rates by Education Level and Type of Orphan, 2008 | 27 |
| 3.9 | Lower Primary School Completion Rate, 2008 | 28 |
| 3.10 | Upper Primary School Completion Rate, 2008 | 29 |
| 3.11 | Reasons for Not Enrolling Children in School by Age, 1998–2008 | 32 |
| 3.12 | Gross Enrollment Rates in Secondary Schools, 1997, 2003, and 2008 | 33 |
| 3.13 | Number of Secondary Schools by Province, 2009 | 34 |
| 3.14 | Enrollment in Public Schools as a Percentage of Total Enrollment, 2009 | 35 |
| 3.15 | Growth in Public and Private Secondary Schools between 2004 and 2009 | 36 |
| 4.1 | Marginal Effect on Enrollment Before and After the Program, by Age Group, 6–18 Years | 43 |
| 5.1 | Education Levels of New Workforce Entrants, 1997, 2003, 2009 | 50 |
| 6.1 | Observed and Projected Distribution of Labor Force by Education Level, 2008 and 2013 | 56 |
| 6.2 | Projected Distribution of Labor Force with Increased Transition Rates at Primary and Secondary Levels, 2013 | 57 |

**Tables**

| | | |
|---|---|---|
| 3.1 | Average Walking Time to School (in minutes) by Educational Level, Consumption Quintile, and Area of Residence, 2008 | 18 |
| 3.2 | School, Teacher, and Enrollment Growth, 2000–10 | 21 |
| 3.3 | Time to Complete a Grade-Level Cycle by Age, 2008 | 23 |
| 3.4 | Repetition Rates by Grade and Year, 1998–2007 | 25 |
| 3.5 | Ratio of Current School Attendance of Orphans vs. Non-Orphans, 2003 and 2008 | 27 |
| 3.6 | Student Survival (in number of students) by Year of Entry into 1st Grade | 29 |
| 3.7 | Households with Positive Education Expenditures (cash and in-kind) by Per Capita Consumption Quintile, 2008 | 31 |
| 5.1 | Structure of Employment, Household vs. Wage, 1997–2009 | 46 |

| | | |
|---|---|---|
| A.1 | Gross Enrollment Rates in Primary by Residence Area and Gender, 1997, 2003, and 2008 (% of population) | 75 |
| A.2 | Net Enrollment Rates in Primary by Residence Area and Gender, 1997, 2003, and 2008 (% of population) | 76 |
| A.3 | Children's Educational Attainment by Age in Primary, 2003 and 2008 | 76 |
| A.4 | Average Transition Rates (% students) | 77 |
| A.5 | Reasons for Never Attending or Dropping Out of School (% of respondents mentioning reason), ages 6–19 Years | 77 |
| A.6 | Reasons for Not Being Enrolled in School, by Age (% respondents mentioning reason), 1998–2008 | 78 |
| A.7 | Dropout Rates in EP1 and EP2 (% respondents), 2003 and 2008 | 78 |
| A.8 | Repetition Rates in EP1 and EP2, by Area of Residence and Gender, 2008 | 79 |
| A.9 | Proportion Spent (per student) on Each Type of Cost in EP1 and EP2, by Area of Residence | 79 |
| A.10 | Per Student Education Expenditure (Mt) by Type of Cost and Consumption Quintile, 2008 | 79 |
| A.11 | Comparison of Annual Per Student Expenditures on Obligatory Contributions (fees), (Mt, constant 2008 prices), 2003 and 2008 | 80 |
| A.12 | Perceptions of Change in Quality of Education since 2004 (% households), by Consumption Quintile | 81 |
| A.13 | Main Reason for Education Improvement (% households citing reason), 2008 | 81 |
| A.14 | Main Reason for Education Worsening (% households citing reason), 2008 | 81 |
| A.15 | Gross Enrollment Rates in Secondary, by Area of Residence and Gender, 1997, 2003, 2008 (% of population) | 82 |
| A.16 | Net Enrollment Rates in Secondary, by Area of Residence and Gender, 1997, 2003, 2008 (% of population) | 82 |
| A.17 | Dropout Rates in ES1 and ES2, by Area of Residence and Gender, 2008 (% of population) | 82 |
| A.18 | Educational Expenditure (Mt/student/year) in ES1, by Consumption Quintile, 2008 | 83 |
| A.19 | Per Student Annual Expenditure (Mt) in ES1, by Area of Residence and Type of Expenditure | 83 |

| | | |
|---|---|---|
| A.20 | Share of the Labor Force (%) with Primary Education, 2003, 2008, and Projected for 2013 | 84 |
| A.21 | Share of the Labor Force (%) with Secondary Education, 2003, 2008, and Projected for 2013 | 86 |
| A.22 | Share of the Labor Force with Education, 2003, 2008, and Alternative Projections for 2013 | 87 |
| C.1 | Effect of the Program for the Exposed Group, Population Ages 6–19 Years | 95 |
| C.2 | Effect of the Program for Each Age, Population 6–19 Years | 98 |

# Acknowledgments

The culmination of a five-year effort, this book is a joint product of the World Bank and the Mozambique Ministries of Education and Culture (MEC) and Planning and Economic Development (MPD). The project was undertaken on behalf of the Government of Mozambique and stakeholders in order to assess household demand for education and the household response to more than a decade of MEC efforts to expand access to education as a cornerstone of Mozambique's economic and social restructuring and development program.

Colleagues from the World Bank, the Government of Mozambique, and the donor community provided valuable support for the study's design and implementation. First, the patient and unfailing support of the Director General of Planning, Dr. Manuel Rego, and his colleagues at the MEC was indispensable. Dr. Rego chaired the project steering committee and provided guidance and support for the study in all phases. Second, Ms. Ana Ruth Menezes at the World Bank office in Maputo, who gave the project technical and moral support, provided the connection between the field teams and the Washington, DC team. Other contributors in Maputo were as follows:

- The National Institute of Education (INDE)—in particular, Dr. Joaquim Matavele and Mr. Flavio Magaia, who led the team of researchers who conducted the initial qualitative assessment;

- Virgulino Nhate at the Ministry of Planning and Rural Development, who helped with the study design;
- Maputo office of KPMG, especially Dr. Paolo Mole, who tirelessly led the team that collected the quantitative household survey data; and
- UNICEF Maputo office staff, who provided technical support throughout the project.

In addition to the authors, the following World Bank staff and consultants contributed to the project: Rui Benfica, Melissa S. Gaal, Anne Louise Grinsted, Elizabeth King, Phillippe Leite, Xiaoyan Liang, David Megill, Hakon Nording, Manolo Sánchez, Kennneth Simler, and the staff of the Maputo office of the World Bank, especially Adelina Mucavele. Harold Alderman, Sandra Beemer, and Patrick McEwan (Wellesley College) provided helpful comments.

Finally, this study could not have gone forward without financial support from the Belgian Poverty Reduction Partnership and the governments of Canada and Sweden through their embassies in Maputo. The study team is grateful for their support, as well as the support of the World Bank through the Research Support Budget.

In the medium term, Mozambique's only hope for exiting from severe poverty and welfare deprivation is an educated and productive population. The study team would like to dedicate this publication to the children of Mozambique, in the hope that through universal education, they will realize a brighter future.

# About the Authors

**Louise Fox** is currently Lead Economist in the Africa Region of the World Bank. During her long career at the Bank, Dr. Fox has been known for her wide-ranging research and analytical interests. Her specialties include analysis of employment and labor markets, poverty and inequality, and the economics of social service delivery, with the overarching theme of the links among policies, outcomes, and poverty reduction. Prior to her current position, Dr. Fox spent 13 years working on issues of labor market adjustment, poverty, and social protection in transition economies, including China and Mongolia, the Baltic States, and Eastern Europe. Before that she researched poverty, inequality, and macroeconomic adjustment in Latin America. Recently she has published on the topics of poverty reduction and inclusive growth, the political economy of poverty reduction, and on employment, labor markets, and labor regulation, all with respect to Sub-Saharan Africa. She has also published in the areas of pension reform, reform of child welfare systems, social protection, public expenditures in the social sectors and poverty reduction, female-headed households and child welfare, stabilization policies and poverty reduction, the social costs of adjustment, and the economic history of poverty and inequality in Brazil. Dr. Fox received a PhD from Vanderbilt University.

**Lucrecia Santibañez** is an Education Economist at the RAND Corporation. Before joining RAND she held positions as Partner and Director of Education Studies at Fundación IDEA in Mexico City, a nonprofit, independent public policy analysis firm. She was also Professor of Public Policy at the Centro de Investigación y Docencia Económicas (CIDE) in Mexico City. Her work focuses on teacher incentives, school-based management programs, and teacher preparation programs. At RAND she is currently involved in the formative evaluation of Summer Learning Programs aimed at increasing learning for disadvantaged students, funded by the Wallace Foundation. She has coauthored books and chapters on teacher incentives and accountability, as well as early childhood development policies. She has received research grants as Principal Investigator or Co-Principal Investigator from Fundacion Mexico Unido, the Bill and Melinda Gates Foundation, the Hewlett Foundation, and the Kellogg Foundation. Her international consulting experience includes projects for the World Bank; the Inter-American Development Bank; and the OECD in Cambodia, El Salvador, Lao PDR, Mexico, Mozambique, Peru, and Qatar. Dr. Santibañez received a PhD in education and an MA in economics, both from Stanford University.

**Vy Thao Nguyen** is an Education Economist at the World Bank's Human Development Network, Education Unit. Her current work focuses on issues of inequalities in education. In her role as an economist, she also provides assistance to the development of the World Bank Group Education Strategy 2020, including a rigorous econometric-based review of the World Bank education portfolio. She has researched women's fertility and labor force participation, as well as financial market liberalization policies and development. Dr. Nguyen received a PhD in economics from American University, Washington, DC.

**Pierre André** is Assistant Professor at the University of Cergy-Pontoise, near Paris. His research focuses on school enrollment decisions in developing countries and the political economy of development. Prior to joining the University of Cergy-Pontoise, he was a consultant in the Africa Region at the World Bank. Dr. André received a PhD from the Paris School of Economics in 2009.

# Abbreviations

| | |
|---|---|
| ADE | Direct Support to Schools (abbreviation for Portuguese) |
| EP1 | *Ensino Primário do 1° Grau* (lower primary grades 1–5) |
| EP2 | *Ensino Primário do 2° Grau* (upper primary grades 6–7) |
| ES1 | *Ensino Secundário do 1° Ciclo* (lower secondary grades 8–10) |
| ES2 | *Ensino Secundário do 2° Ciclo* (upper secondary grades 11–12) |
| GER | gross enrollment rate |
| GoM | Government of Mozambique |
| HE | household enterprise |
| IAF | Inquérito aos Agregados Familiares |
| INE | Instituto Nacional de Estatística |
| IOF | Inquérito aos Orcamentos Familiares |
| MEC | Ministry of Education and Culture |
| MICS | Multiple Indicator Cluster Survey |
| MOE | Ministry of Education |
| MSMEs | micro, small, and medium enterprises |
| Mt | metical (Mozambique currency) |
| NER | net enrollment rate |
| NPS | National Panel Survey |

| | |
|---|---|
| PARPA | Plan of Action for the Reduction of Absolute Poverty (Portuguese) |
| PSIA | Poverty and Social Impact Analysis |
| SSA | Sub-Saharan Africa |

**CHAPTER 1**

# Introduction

In 1994, after the end of the civil war and the first free elections, Mozambique was an extremely poor country with a decimated infrastructure, a weak economy, and fragile institutions. It has since been successful at restoring growth and improving welfare. The GDP per capita has been growing approximately 5 percent annually since 2006,[1] and the portion of the population living on less than US$1.25 per day (extreme poverty) declined from an estimated 81 percent in 1996–97 to 60 percent in 2008.[2] Although Mozambique remains a poor country, much has improved in the last 20 years (see box 1.1).

Sound economic policies have contributed to Mozambique's strong economic growth in the last two decades. Broad-based, labor-intensive private-sector growth was efficient at poverty reduction until 2003 (Fox et al. 2008). At the same time, investments in social and economic infrastructure extended access to public services, reduced welfare inequalities, and supported the livelihood of the average Mozambican. Since 2003, high growth has been sustained by a combination of natural resource extraction financed by foreign direct investment and sector service expansion, while the agricultural sector, which employs the majority of the labor force, has experienced slower growth. Income growth in rural areas, in which more than 60 percent of Mozambicans live, has been sluggish. The key

> **Box 1.1**
>
> ## Mozambique At a Glance
>
> Mozambique is located on the east coast of southern Africa and is part of Sub-Saharan Africa (SSA). It is divided into 10 provinces (see box 1.2) with the capital in Maputo. Mozambique declared independence from Portugal in 1975. A prolonged civil war followed, lasting until 1992. The current population is 22 million, of which 46 percent is under 14 years of age. Only 3 percent of the population is over age 65. Thirty-eight percent of the population lives in urban areas. The country currently ranks 165th in the world on the Human Development Indicators index, with a value of 0.284 (SSA average is 0.389). Life expectancy at birth is 42 years, one of the lowest in the world. The country has one of the highest infant mortality rates (115 per 1,000), as well as high child mortality (168 per 1,000) and HIV adult prevalence (11.5 percent).
>
> *Sources:* Focus Africa, http://focusafrica.gov.in/Country_at_glance_Mozambique.html. World Development Indicators, http://data.worldbank.org/data-catalog/world-development-indicators. HDI data from United Nations Development Programme, http://hdrstats.undp.org/en/countries/profiles/MOZ.html

development challenge for Mozambique is to further accelerate the country's economic development by reshaping its growth patterns to benefit a larger segment of the population.

## The Education Challenge

After winning the first multi-party election in 1994, the Mozambique Government faced an enormous education deficit. High absolute poverty levels and difficulties in accessing areas outside provincial capitals during the 20-year civil war caused enrollment to plummet, with gross enrollment in primary school at only 50 percent and net enrollment below 40 percent. Infrastructure was in very poor shape, and schools were completely absent in many rural areas. Schools often lacked inputs (teachers, books, supplies, and the like). Many teachers were not qualified to teach. The objective of Government policy since the end of the civil war has been to provide quality education for all with a focus on primary education. Government strategy focused on achieving universal primary education (EP1 and EP2; see box 1.3), primarily by expanding the infrastructure network and also by improving the efficiency of resource use.

By 2004, Mozambique had done a heroic job of improving access to lower and upper primary schools through sustained investment in

**Box 1.2**

**Map of Provinces in Mozambique**

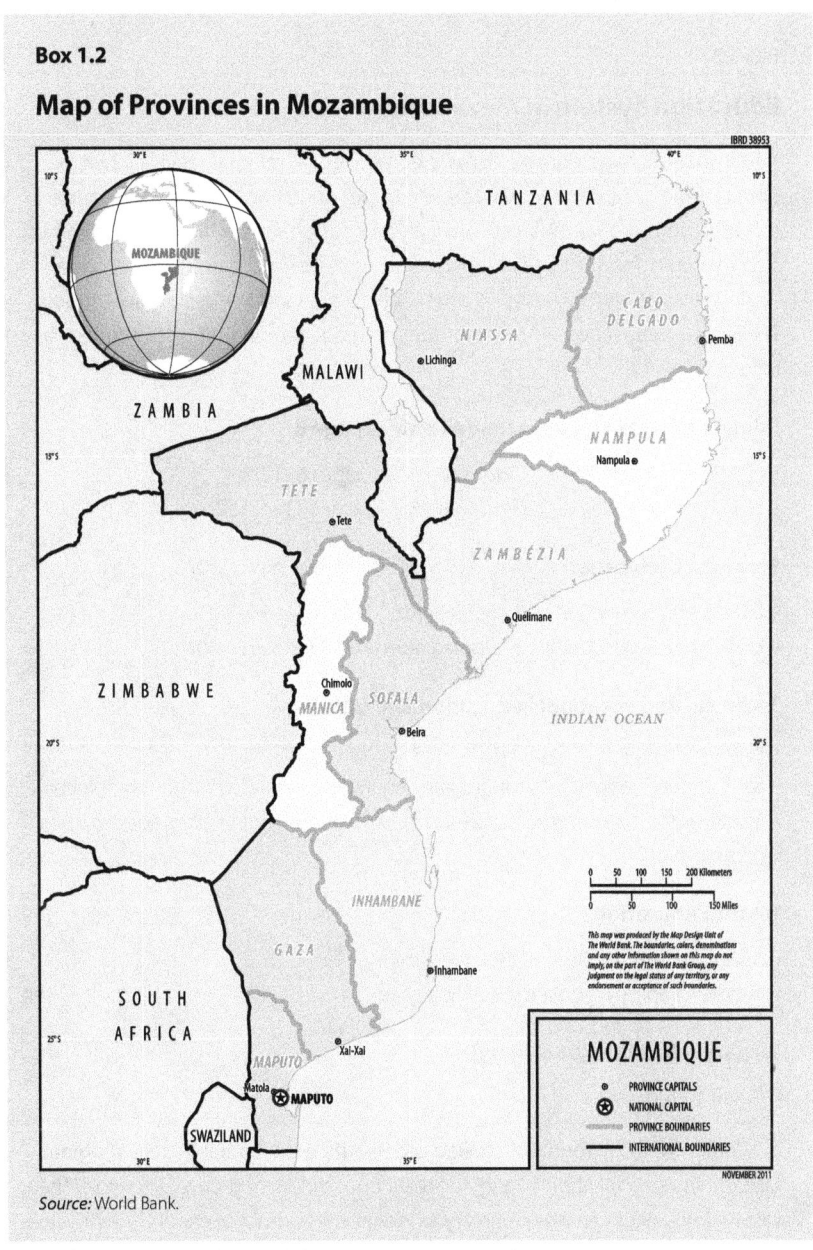

*Source:* World Bank.

education. Since 2000, the Government has allocated an average of 20 percent of revenue, about 5 percent of GDP, to the education sector (World Bank 2005). Between 2000 and 2003, the number of schools increased significantly, with the addition of 1,005 lower primary schools and 428 upper primary schools (MEC 2010). This supply expansion was

**Box 1.3**

# Education System in Mozambique

Mozambique's basic education cycle comprises two primary levels: lower and upper primary. Students who complete upper primary can go on to secondary school. There are various technical and vocational education and training opportunities for graduates of lower and upper primary, or lower secondary. Tertiary education (university) is open only to graduates of secondary schools. The levels of education in Mozambique and grade requirements for entry are as follows:

### Primary education with intended entry at age 6

- EP1 (*Ensino Primário do 1º Grau*): grades 1–5 (ages 6–10)
- EP2 (*Ensino Primário do 2º Grau*): grades 6–7 (ages 11–12)

### Secondary education

- ES1 (*Ensino Secundário do 1º Ciclo*): grades 8–10 (ages 13–15)
- ES2 (*Ensino Secundário do 2º Ciclo*): grades 11–12 (ages 16–17)

### Technical and vocational education and training

- Elementary (grade 5 required, 2–3-year programs)
- Basic (grade 7 required, 3-year program, equivalent to grade 10 upon completion)
- Medium (grade 10 required, 2-year program, equivalent to grade 12 upon completion)

### Teacher education

- Basic (grade 7 required, 3-year program)
- Middle (grade 10 required, 1-year program)

### Tertiary education (university)

- Grade 12 required

In addition to these formal schooling grades, there is an adult literacy program. Mozambique's education system includes both public and private schools. The vast majority (95 percent) of primary students attend public schools. The private sector, however, plays an important role in upper secondary (ES2), with around a third of students attending private schools.

*Source:* MEC 2010.

met with overwhelming demand. Gross enrollment rose from 67.7 percent in 1997 to 100 percent in 2003 at the lower primary level, in part a result of children past primary school age who were able to enroll for the first time. The increase was similarly high for the upper primary level, from 34 percent in 1997 to 57 percent in 2003 (Fox et al. 2008).

But the improvement in enrollment still left a large number of children out of school, in particular Mozambique's most vulnerable populations: girls and children in rural areas. While physical access improved, efficiency did not, and retention and completion rates were also dismally low. In 2003, only 40 percent of school-age children completed lower primary school and 17 percent completed upper primary school (Valerio et al. 2006). Unlike most African countries, in Mozambique, entrance into successively higher levels of schooling is not based on national examinations, but on a student's grades and age. Among students with the same grades, those who are younger, and therefore either started on time or did not repeat a grade, are given priority (Handa, Simler, and Harrower 2004). While low coverage rates as well as low education efficiency could have many causes, education authorities, policy makers, parents, and school leaders all perceived that direct costs as well as indirect (opportunity) costs of education were a significant barrier.

To better understand the key bottlenecks to increased enrollment, in 2004 the World Bank with other donors and the Mozambique Government prepared a Poverty and Social Impact Analysis (PSIA) on the issue of fee reform in primary school (World Bank 2005). In addition, the Bank conducted a successful pilot phase of the "Direct Support to Schools" program, or ADE (Portuguese). Both projects contributed to a greater understanding of the demand-side and supply-side barriers undercutting access to primary education, particularly for rural and other disadvantaged populations, and informed policy reforms.

With support from donors and key stakeholders, the Government in 2004–05 addressed the causes of low enrollment by enacting an important set of reforms as follows:

1. ***Reduction in direct costs for households and provision of free textbooks.*** National tuition and other fees in primary education were abolished and textbooks were provided free of charge to schools.
2. ***Increased funding at the school level.*** Schools received additional funds channeled through the "Direct Support to Schools" (ADE) program. ADE provides funds on a capitation basis directly to primary schools for non-salary expenses.

3. *New curriculum.* A new curriculum was introduced, organized into three main blocks (grades 1–2, grades 3–5, and grades 6–7). Options of developing up to 20 percent of the curriculum at the subnational level (district or province) and for teaching in the native tongue for grades 1 and 2 were provided.
4. *Semiautomatic promotion.* As part of the curriculum reform, pupils receive automatic promotion within each grade block. Promotion between blocks is based on school exams. In practice, there is no exam to enter grade 3.

In addition, the Government's investment program continued to expand the network of lower and upper primary schools through school construction and teacher training.

In 2006, the Mozambique Ministry of Education and Culture (MEC) asked the World Bank to conduct a deeper analysis of barriers to enrollment in primary and secondary education. In particular MEC sought assistance in evaluating the success of the reforms in primary education financing to date and in formulating new policies and initiatives to reduce the barriers the poorest households faced in accessing primary and secondary education. The Bank agreed to finance and supervise both a qualitative and quantitative study.

This report provides the key findings from the World Bank's quantitative study. In addition, it uses the findings from the qualitative study (cited here as World Bank 2007) throughout to provide relevant information and evidence to support its main messages.

## Organization of This Report

The report opens with a brief description of the conceptual framework that guided the analysis as well as the data used. The next chapter presents the analysis of changes in household behavior and educational outcomes related to the implementation of the reforms, at both the primary and secondary levels. The descriptive nature of this analysis does not allow for inferences regarding the *effects* of the reforms on enrollment and demand for education. The following chapter presents the results of an econometric impact analysis of the reforms to quantify the magnitude of the effects on enrollment.

In considering priorities for the future, the Government is paying increasing attention to the impact of the investments in education on growth, jobs, and poverty reduction, as measured by increased earnings from employment, and particularly by improving opportunities for the labor force to move to higher productivity activities and livelihoods. The next chapter presents the results on the changing structure of employment in Mozambique between 2003 and 2008, the impacts of education on employment opportunities, and the implications of these changes for education policy. The final chapter integrates the education and labor force analyses and provides strategic recommendations as Mozambique continues to improve educational outcomes, particularly for those population groups that have had the most difficulty entering and remaining in school.

## Notes

1. http://data.worldbank.org/indicator/NY.GDP.PCAP.KD.ZG
2. Adjusted for purchasing power parity (PPP) at 2005 international prices. Data are from World Development Indicators, http://data.worldbank.org/data-catalog/world-development-indicators. Poverty indicators, http://data.worldbank.org/indicator/SI.POV.DDAY/countries

## References

Fox, L., R. M. Benfica, M. Ehrenpreis, M. S. Gaal, H. Nordang, and D. Owen. 2008. *Beating the Odds: Sustaining Inclusion in a Growing Economy: A Mozambique Poverty, Gender, and Social Assessment.* Washington, DC: World Bank.

Handa, S., K. L. Simler, and S. Harrower. 2004. "Human Capital, Household Welfare, and Children's Schooling in Mozambique." Research Report 134. International Food Policy Institute, Washington, DC.

MEC (Ministério da Educação e Cultura). 2010. "Os resultados do sector através dos principais indicadores." (Progress Report). Ministry of Education and Culture, Government of Mozambique, Maputo, Mozambique.

Valerio, A., E. Bardasi, A. Chambal, and M. F. Lobo. 2006. "Mozambique: School Fees and Primary School Enrollment Retention." In *Poverty and Social Impact Analysis of Reforms: Lessons and Examples from Implementation*, 93–148, ed. A. Coudouel, A. A. Dani, and S. Paternostro. Washington, DC: World Bank.

World Bank. 2005. "Poverty and Social Impact Analysis: Primary School Enrollment and Retention—The Impact of School Fees." World Bank, Washington, DC.

———. 2007. "PSIA II—Follow-up Study of Primary Education and Baseline Study of Secondary Education, Mozambique." World Bank, Washington, DC.

**CHAPTER 2**

# Conceptual Framework and Data

In standard economic theory, following Kanbur (2008), a household's decision to send each child to school depends on the costs and benefits of schooling. Costs include direct expenses (tuition, fees, books, uniforms, and so on) and indirect expenses (foregone earnings). Benefits include the economic returns, that is, income or future earnings, from obtaining schooling of a given quality.

Quality may affect returns to schooling and perhaps even costs. Higher quality schools could be more expensive (higher tuition, more books, and so on), although in a completely public system this might not be the case. They can also affect the indirect costs of schooling by making greater demands on the child's time (for example, by expecting higher attendance, offering more classes, and so on). Non-economic preferences on schooling of children, preferences regarding present versus future consumption and access to credit, may also affect the decision to send a child to school (Kanbur 2008).

Government intervention in education is usually justified on the grounds that, left to themselves, private individuals (or households) would tend to underinvest in education, leading to less efficient and inequitable schooling outcomes for society. This is particularly a problem when parents are determining the future education level for children, as the benefits of the investment are long term but the costs are incurred in the short term. Given these constraints, households must be motivated to send their children to school, either by reducing the cost to the household and improving access or by increasing the returns, either through increases in quality for a given cost of education or through improvements in the economy and household incomes so that the cost of education is not such a burden and the rewards are more accessible.

## Education Supply and Demand

Following this conceptual framework, education systems can be constrained by supply or demand, and the ability to identify which is the most binding of these constraints could help governments plan more strategic actions (Kanbur 2008). A system is supply-constrained if it cannot meet demand with available school spaces. And a supply-constrained system might not have enough places to even meet a constant demand. In this case, the first priority would be to build more schools. The "malleable" nature of education (that is, the willingness to accept larger class sizes), however, makes it difficult to ascertain at what point a system has become or has ceased to be supply-constrained (see box 2.1).

In a demand-constrained system, on the other hand, the number of existing school spaces (at fixed quality) exceeds the demand for these places. Schools exist, but children do not attend because something (unaffordable fees, long distance to school, family need for the child's labor, belief that the child is not ready for school, socio-cultural views, among others) makes households choose not to send the child to school. If the system is demand-constrained, there is no point in spending resources on increasing the number of school places (Kanbur 2008).

It is possible that the system is supply-constrained with regard to a given type of school (for example, high schools or higher quality elementary schools). The implication would be the same: build or expand more of these types of schools or improve existing schools so they join this category.

A system could be both demand- and supply-constrained at the same time, for example, if urban areas are demand-constrained while rural areas are supply-constrained. Or education for boys might be supply-constrained, but girls might not be sent to school even if there are places for them because of additional important socio-cultural and economic factors. In Mozambique early marriage or pregnancy among girls has a negative effect on their schooling. Initiation rites for boys and girls

> **Box 2.1**
>
> ## The "Malleable" Nature of Education Supply
>
> One feature of education systems that complicates supply and demand analyses is the "malleable" nature of education: supply of education can accommodate rising demand, as long as there is a willingness to accept higher class sizes. Often, education access can be expanded mainly through class size flexibility. There is no consensus, however, on the effects of class sizes on student performance or other indicators of quality.[1] While extremely large class size is probably not a good idea, over or under capacity is likely to be a function of what an education system is willing to accept as a suitable standard and how much teachers are supported, through preparation and other resources, to handle. Some education systems function well with 40 students per teacher, others set 20 students per teacher as a more desirable goal. Without a firm standard on class sizes, exploring whether a system is supply- or demand-constrained is difficult because it is difficult to establish the point at which the system becomes truly supply-constrained.
>
> *Source:* Authors.
> 1. For a recent review of this literature see Bascia 2010, http://www.cea-ace.ca/publication/reducing-class-size-what-do-we-know.

also tend to have a negative impact, with families often preferring to matriculate their children after they finish the initiation rites (World Bank 2007). In other cases, after girls pass through the initiation rites, they may see themselves as adults and no longer see the need for formal education.

Another particularly vulnerable group that is likely to be demand-constrained is orphans. The increasing number of children who have lost one or both parents is a grim effect of the HIV/AIDS epidemic. In 2007 twice as many children had lost one or both parents to HIV/AIDS than in 2003 (Fox et al. 2008). The well-being of orphaned children almost always suffers, which has potentially negative consequences for their socioeconomic status in adulthood. All of these factors are more prevalent in more remote rural areas, where physical access is poorest, further adding to the constraints to schooling of children living in those regions.

If the government has a fixed amount to spend on education, with the objective of increasing the number of children who gain skills prior to entering the labor force, how should the resources be spent? This was the problem facing Mozambique in 2004–05 as it formulated its next education strategy. Policies had to be targeted to specific populations or needs to ensure that educational objectives were reached. But priorities also had to be set: given a number of policy choices, the Government had to decide where to intervene first. Using the conceptual framework described above, the Government's policies can be classified as (1) continuing to address the supply constraints in rural areas, while (2) trying to relieve the demand constraints by lowering direct costs to households, and (3) at the same time, raising quality through the new curriculum, and (4) increasing quality and efficiency through the semiautomatic promotion policy, which would reduce repetition rates, thus reducing pupil-teacher ratios.

Because one of the justifications for government intervention in education is equity, an analysis of the reforms should include a review of which income groups were expected to benefit. Supply-side policies for remote areas should be unambiguously pro-poor, as poorer households lived farther from schools in 2003. Reduction of fees normally benefits all households equally but is generally considered pro-poor, because the poor have less income to spend on sending their children to school. Likewise, reductions in fees should favor vulnerable groups for which the household is less likely to invest in education. The quality improvements should benefit all households, although if poor children were going to schools with the highest student-teacher ratios, this policy might benefit them more than wealthier students.

The analysis below uses the conceptual framework to assess first, if the reforms appear to have had their desired effect on supply, demand, and quality, and second, if they did, which groups of households and children benefitted. The framework is used to discuss policy options for Mozambique's next set of reforms, which will have the objectives of further expanding access to education, while at the same time striving to improve efficiency and quality.

## Data and Sources

The analysis presented in this report used data from six different sources (see box 2.2 for a description and some sampling issues for the surveys used). In addition, it used school census data for various years, provided by the Mozambique Ministry of Education and Culture. Any other data sources are noted in the text.

**Box 2.2**

## Description of Survey Data Used in the Analysis

- *IAF for 1996–97.* The *Inquérito aos Agregados Familiares* (IAF) is the first nationally representative household income and consumption survey conducted after the cessation of hostilities. It was conducted by the National Institute of Statistics. The survey contains some limited education information regarding enrollment and attendance status.
- *IAF 2002–03.* The *Inquérito aos Agregados Familiares* (IAF) is a national household income and expenditure survey conducted from July 2002 to June 2003, which covers about 8,700 households and 44,000 individuals. It contains information similar to the 1996–97 survey on expenditures and characteristics of Mozambican households. As in 1996–97, it includes a short education module and some questions about education expenditures.
- *IOF 2008-09.* The *Inquérito aos Orcamentos Familiares* (IOF) is the third national household income and expenditure survey, conducted from October 2008 to July 2009. It contains information similar to the IAF surveys on expenditures and characteristics of Mozambican households.
- *NPS 2008.* The National Panel Survey (NPS) was designed as a longitudinal survey based on a subsample of the IAF 2002–03. The 2008 NPS is only representative of the households in the 2003 subsample that still live in the same location or district and had children 17 years of age or younger in 2002–03 (it was too expensive to track households that moved outside the district). At the national level, the NPS sample represents 78.9 percent of the subsample, or about 20 percent of the 2003 households. Rural areas are more stable, covering 83.1 percent compared to 69.9 percent for urban areas. An ex-post weighting scheme was applied to partially correct for the attrition. It was found that the level of precision was satisfactory for most indicators by urban and rural stratum. The number of observations for secondary students was low, as expected, especially for the rural stratum. The NPS 2008 questionnaire is rich in information covering different topics, including an education history module that asks respondents to recall education decisions (enrollment, dropout, highest grade completed, and so on) for each child in the household going back to 1998. The information on household consumption, education expenditures, educational attainment, and household incomes and economic activity is not directly comparable to the 2002–03 survey.

*(continued next page)*

> **Box 2.2** *(continued)*
>
> - **MICS 2008.** The Multiple Indicator Cluster Survey (MICS) was conducted in 2008 by the *Instituto Nacional de Estatística* (INE) with technical and financial support from UNICEF. This national level, multi-purpose household survey was carried out by 25 teams of interviewers from August to December 2008. Data entry began in October 2008 and was completed in April 2009. MICS collected data from nearly 14,000 households across the 10 provinces of the country plus Maputo City. The survey used a two-stage sample design: in the first stage, enumeration areas were selected in each province; in the second stage, households were selected in each area. The MICS sample was designed to be statistically representative at national and provincial levels, as well as by key background characteristics of respondents, including urban and rural areas, wealth quintile, and education level.
> - **PSIA II.** To gain additional insight and help design the questionnaire for the NPS, a qualitative study was undertaken in 2007 under World Bank guidance to collect contextual data on the impact of the primary school reforms and on secondary education. The study collected interview and focus group data from 30 schools in 12 districts and 4 provinces in Mozambique. Two data collection methods were used: individual interviews using semi-structured interview guides and focus groups. Teachers, parents, MEC officials, school administrators, and other key actors were interviewed over a period of 5 weeks in March and April 2007. The study was used to provide early feedback to the MEC and to guide the construction of the NPS questionnaire.
>
> *Source:* Authors, http://microdatalib.worldbank.org/index.php/catalog/2154.

## References

Bascia, Nina. 2010. *Reducing Class Size: What Do We Know?* Canadian Education Association, Toronto, Onatario, Canada. http://www.cea-ace.ca/publication/reducing-class-size-what-do-we-know.

Fox, L., R. M. Benfica, M. Ehrenpreis, M. S. Gaal, H. Nordang, and D. Owen. 2008. *Beating the Odds: Sustaining Inclusion in a Growing Economy: A Mozambique Poverty, Gender, and Social Assessment.* Washington, DC: World Bank.

Kanbur, R. 2008. "Intergenerationalities: Some Educational Questions on Quality, Quantity and Opportunity." Working Paper 2009-107. Cornell University, Ithaca, NY.

World Bank. 2007. "PSIA II—Follow-up Study of Primary Education and Baseline Study of Secondary Education, Mozambique." World Bank, Washington, DC.

CHAPTER 3

# Analysis of the Effects of the 2004–05 Reforms: Outputs and Outcomes

This chapter reports on the analysis of the survey data on enrollment, cost of education, and efficiency. It highlights changes and trends in enrollment from 1997 to 2003 and 2003 to 2008. Moreover, it takes advantage of the National Panel Survey (NPS) Education History Module to investigate reasons for not entering school and for dropping out. It also provides a wealth of information regarding school fees and costs, including whether they decreased between 2003 and 2008. Finally, the data include variables describing household consumption, which allows analysis by economic (consumption) quintile, in addition to the standard gender and area of residence groupings. Additional tables can be found in Appendix A.

## Primary Education

*Primary school reforms were accompanied by a surge in enrollment at the lower and upper primary levels.*

Enrollment in lower primary continued to increase after the reforms of 2004–05, especially in rural areas and for girls (appendix table A1). Gross enrollment for rural girls jumped from 86 to 99 percent—almost equal to the national average of 104 percent. Reflecting the tendency to start children in school late, the net enrollment rates were much lower. But rural areas still posted a strong gain in net enrollment, from 58 to 69 percent.

Enrollment in upper primary also continued to increase after 2004, but at a slower rate than in the previous period (see figure 3.1).[1] Enrollment in upper primary still grew faster than lower primary, indicating that there had been serious constraints to access at this level. After 2004, the Government more than doubled the number of upper primary teachers and schools. The alleviation of supply constraints is likely to be at least partly responsible for the upper primary gross enrollment rate (GER) going from 57 percent in 2003 to over 78 percent in 2008.

However, the pupil-teacher ratio in upper primary decreased by 17 percent between 2004 and 2010, despite the still fairly low enrollment rates. This suggests that (1) either the system became supply constrained at this point at a given (fixed) quality (that is, schools were not willing to increase pupil-teacher ratios further), or, more likely (2) the new supply of schools absorbed the fraction of the population that had been able to afford upper primary, plus a proportion for whom the 2004–05 reforms made a marginal difference in their willingness to send children to upper primary (perhaps by encouraging them to remain in lower primary), complete this level, and transition further.

Figure 3.2 shows enrollment rates by consumption quintile using NPS data.

**Figure 3.1 Gross Enrollment Rates in Primary Schools, 1997, 2003, 2008**

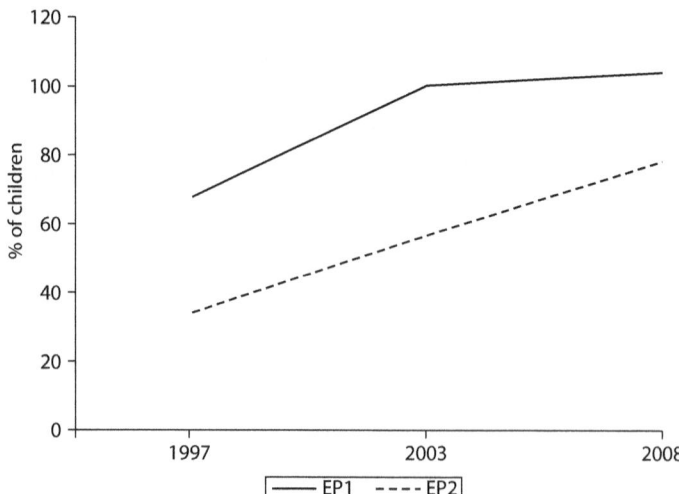

*Sources:* IAF 1996–97, IAF 2002–03 (from Fox et al. 2008); MICS 2008.
*Note:* Rates are consistent, using official ages prior to the 2006 change (6–11 EP1, 12–13 EP2).

**Figure 3.2  Age-Relevant Enrollment Rate by Consumption Quintile, 2008**

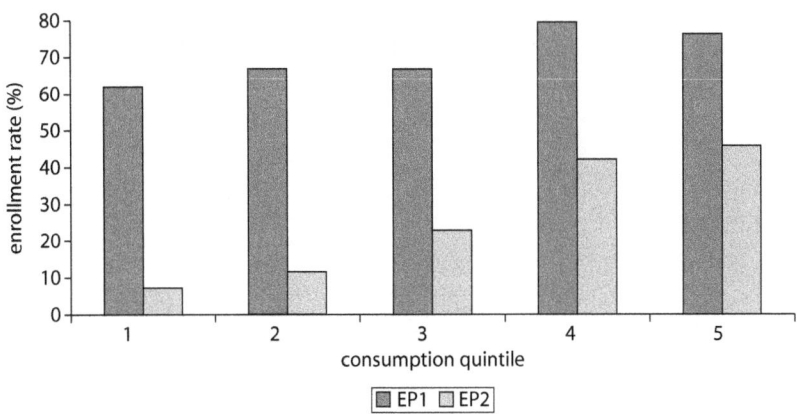

*Source:* NPS 2008.
*Note:* Age groups are 6–11 in EP1 and 12–13 in EP2 using official ages prior to the 2006 change.

Lower primary enrollment rates are mostly similar across quintiles. This is noteworthy because it is at this level that fees and overall costs tend to be lower and the network of schools is much larger, particularly in rural areas. Reflecting mostly equal access on the supply side, table 3.1 shows that travel (walking) times to the nearest EP1 school are fairly similar across consumption quintiles. Thus it suggests that the remaining constraints households face in enrolling children in EP1 are probably not on the supply side and not directly income related, but are more related to other demand-side factors.

In upper primary, on the other hand, where fees and costs are higher and supply is lower (particularly in rural areas), a much higher proportion of children from better-off families are enrolled in school. Travel times to the nearest EP2 school are much higher for children in rural areas and for children from the bottom two quintiles. Even though national school fees were abolished in both lower and upper primary, figure 3.2 suggests significant barriers to access remain for low-income families. For these households, the 2004–05 reforms were insufficient to generate much more enrollment traction particularly since other demand- and supply-side constraints remain.

> *The 2004 reforms appear to have lowered the direct costs to households of attending primary education, particularly lower primary.*

**Table 3.1  Average Walking Time to School (in minutes) by Educational Level, Consumption Quintile, and Area of Residence, 2008**

| Grade level | Consumption quintile | | | | | Residence area | | |
|---|---|---|---|---|---|---|---|---|
| | 1 | 2 | 3 | 4 | 5 | Urban | Rural | National |
| EP1 | 28 | 33 | 26 | 31 | 26 | 22 | 32 | 29 |
| EP2 | 45 | 44 | 41 | 38 | 34 | 27 | 48 | 40 |
| ES1 | 62 | 47 | 63 | 38 | 46 | 48 | 51 | 48 |
| ES2 | 20 | 197 | 67 | 48 | 68 | 64 | 103 | 74 |
| National | 31 | 36 | 32 | 34 | 40 | 33 | 35 | 34 |

*Source:* NPS 2008.
*Note 1:* "Average walking time" in NPS refers to the average walking time to school for an individual in minutes. The totals column uses information from all cases. Totals differ upon breakdown for rural/urban because of missing observations in the rural/urban variable for a few households.
*Note 2:* "Average walking time" in NPS is different from the IAF variable, since IAF 2002–03 computed an average walking distance to the nearest school in the district (not necessarily the school being attended). They are not directly comparable.

The NPS data show that the direct costs of attending school were lower in 2008. While fees did not disappear, the fees reported (mandatory plus voluntary) decreased for most households between 2003 and 2008. Focus groups conducted in 2007 confirmed this, reporting that since 2004 parents reported direct school costs had decreased because of the abolition of fees and the provision of textbooks and other school material (World Bank 2007).

The poorest families saw fees decline the most (see figure 3.3). For households struggling to stay out of poverty, the reform had less effect. (It is important to note that, in Mozambique, poverty extends up to the middle of the population distribution, that is, most families in Mozambique are poor.) But this comparison must be taken with caution as the questions in the two surveys were phrased slightly differently. However, it does suggest that EP1 fees decreased in this time period for the lowest two quintiles, while remaining constant and even increasing for the middle and upper quintiles.

## Costs Affect Access

In upper primary, obligatory contributions fell significantly for almost all quintiles, except the middle one (see figure 3.4).[2] However, absolute numbers suggest these fees are still high. According to this survey data, a household in the lowest quintile pays more than double the obligatory contributions in EP2 than it does in EP1.

**Figure 3.3 Comparison of Annual Per Student Expenditures on Obligatory Contributions (fees) in EP1, 2003 and 2008 (constant 2008 prices)**

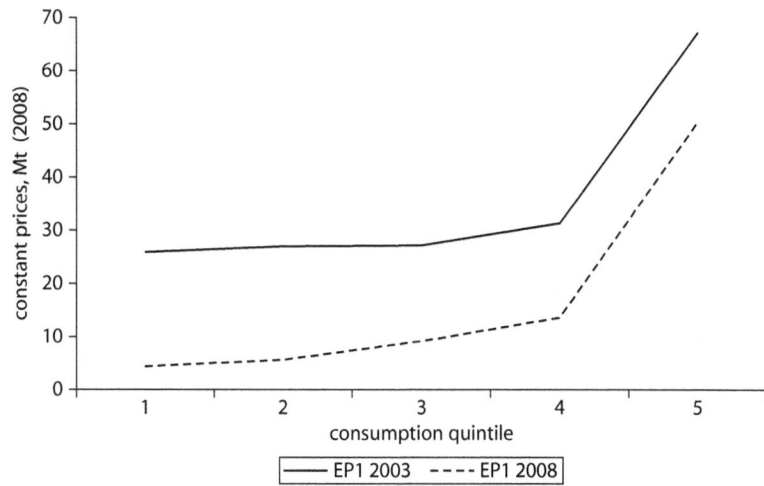

*Sources:* IAF 2002–03, World Bank 2005, NPS 2008. In 2008, fees were set at the local level and are labeled "obligatory" if households identified them as such.

*Note:* Regarding calculation of fees: In 2002–03 obligatory fees includes *propina e matricula* (tuition and registration fee). In 2008, they include *propina* (tuition), *matricula* (registration fee), and other mandatory fees (worksheets, exam fee, and so on). For the constant price conversion, 2008 is the base year. To calculate other years' price indices, the series of average consumer data for 2000–10 (base 2000) from IMF was used.

Why do fees remain, and at such high levels, even after they were abolished by the national government? This was indeed one of the surprising results of the NPS survey. Data from the survey and focus groups lead to the following conclusions:

- The policy does not forbid the school parent-teacher organization from levying fees, and this is what seems to be happening. Sometimes fees were levied to cover a specific issue (for example, replacing broken windows); while in other cases they were levied to top up the recurrent cost budget (for example, to pay for the services of guards, extra pay for teachers, or supplemental materials).
- Clearly, school management and the communities they serve perceived the resources provided from the national budget to be insufficient. At the same time, there is no tracking or regulation of locally imposed fees at either the district, province, or national level.
- For lower income families, especially in EP1, the majority of the fees reported were labeled "voluntary," indicating awareness at the local level of the burden that fees may pose for some households.

**Figure 3.4  Comparison of Annual Per Student Expenditures on Obligatory Contributions (fees) in EP2, 2003 and 2008 (constant 2008 prices)**

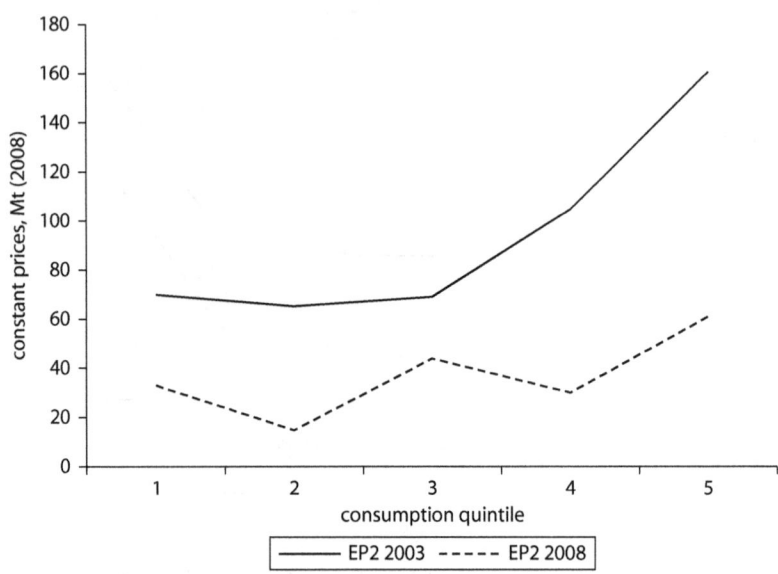

*Sources:* IAF 2002–03, World Bank 2005, and NPS 2008. In 2008, fees were set at the local level and are labeled "obligatory" if households identified them as such.
*Note:* Regarding calculation of fees: In 2002–03 obligatory fees include *propina e matricula* (tuition and registration fee). In 2008, they include *propina* (tuition), *matricula* (registration fee), and other mandatory fees (worksheets, exam fee, and so on). For the constant price conversion 2008 is the base year. To calculate other years' price indices, the series of average consumer data for 2000–10 (base 2000) from IMF was used.

## 2004 Reforms

> *A program of school construction and hiring of teachers accompanied the 2004 reforms, leading to a considerably higher supply of schools and classes in both lower and upper primary.*

The 2004 reforms were enacted along with a program of school construction and teacher hiring that had begun in 2000 that considerably increased the number of schools and classes taught. The fact that these two government programs happened at the same time complicates the evaluation of the 2004–05 policy. Furthermore, because pupil-teacher ratios are flexible to accommodate fluctuations in enrollment, it is difficult to ascertain when schools are over-capacity or under-capacity, unless some external quality benchmarks are used.

Table 3.2 shows school, teacher, and enrollment trends for the period 2000–03, when the policy focus was on school expansion, and the period after 2004, when the school financing reforms were implemented.

**Table 3.2  School, Teacher, and Enrollment Growth, 2000–10**

| Primary level/factor | Growth 2000–03 (%) | Growth 2004–10 (%) |
|---|---|---|
| EP1 | | |
| Schools | 14 | 29 |
| Teachers | 49 | 58 |
| Enrollment | 49 | 70 |
| Pupil-teacher ratio | 0 | 8 |
| EP2 | | |
| Schools | 82 | 215 |
| Teachers | 130 | 147 |
| Enrollment | 265 | 104 |
| Pupil-teacher ratio | 59 | −17 |

*Source:* Author estimations using MEC 2010 data.

In EP1, the number of schools increased from 7,072 in 2000 to 8,077 in 2003 and 10,444 in 2010 (MEC 2010). After 2004, however, when the demand-side reforms kicked in, enrollment rose faster than the accompanying increases in teachers and schools. The pupil-teacher ratio increased 8 percent during this time.

In upper primary (EP2), the number of schools and teachers almost doubled between 2000 and 2003. Admittedly, the high percentage growth figures are partly the result of the low initial stock of upper primary schools in the period of reference. In 2000, there were only 522 EP2 schools in Mozambique. By 2003, there were 950 and by 2010, there were 2,990 (MEC 2010).

> *Despite spectacular growth in the past decade, efficiency rates remain low and many children who should be in school are not.*

Mozambique should be commended for having made lower primary education more accessible to families across the income spectrum. It should also be commended for its great strides in making upper primary more accessible too, even though many upper primary schools remain beyond the reach of the poorest families.

## Effects of Late Entry, Long Completion Times

Many children who should be in school are not and children take longer than expected to successfully complete an education level, and most do not complete the level. This is summarized in the net enrollment rate (NER). NERs improved in lower primary from 39 percent in 1997 to 72 percent in 2008 (see figure 3.5), likely primarily driven by more children starting

**Figure 3.5 Net Enrollment Rates in Primary Schools, 1997, 2003, 2008**

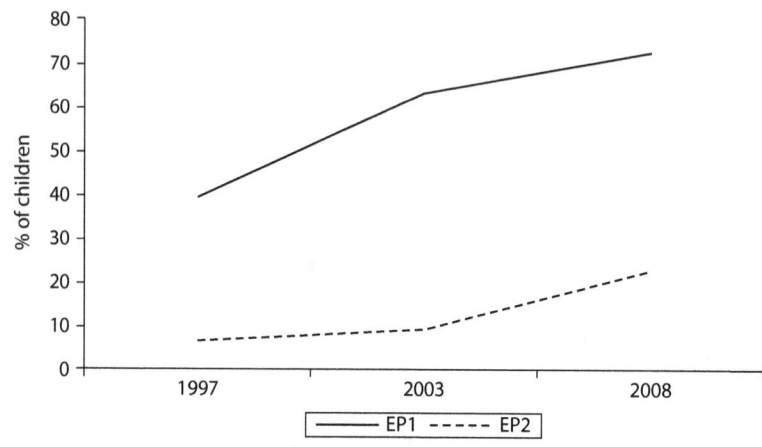

*Sources:* MICS 2008, IAF 2002–03, IAF 1996–97.
*Note:* Rates are consistent, using official ages prior to the 2006 change (6–11 EP1, 12–13 EP2).

on time. In upper primary, NERs are better now than they were in 1997, but they remain very low. In 2008, only 22.6 percent of age-relevant children in Mozambique were enrolled at this level.

The low NERs highlight the difficulty of keeping children in school in Mozambique. Close to 80 percent of 11-year-olds attend school, but only 10 percent are attending upper primary, their official age-relevant level (see figure 3.6). Although the proportion of children attending school at most ages has improved since 2003, even among 12-year-olds, the proportion attending EP2 in 2008 was only around 20 percent. And most 13-year-olds, who should be in secondary school, remain in lower primary.

Late entry into school is related to high dropout rates and low efficiency rates (Wils 2004). Late entry into schooling, however, does not itself necessarily lead to less education completed. It is possible that the lost opportunity for learning from a delay in starting school might be partially offset by improved school readiness, that is, how developmentally ready children are to learn, work and function successfully in school.[3] Other authors have suggested that the negative consequences of late enrollment are seen mostly in future earnings and wealth. In their study of Ghana, Glewwe and Jacoby (1995) suggest that for each year of delay in primary school entry in that country, a child could lose around 6 percent of lifetime wealth.

The figures in table 3.3, however, suggest that delayed entry is common among children in Mozambique. Among children who complete a grade

**Figure 3.6 Children Attending EP1 and EP2 Schools by Age, 2003 and 2008**

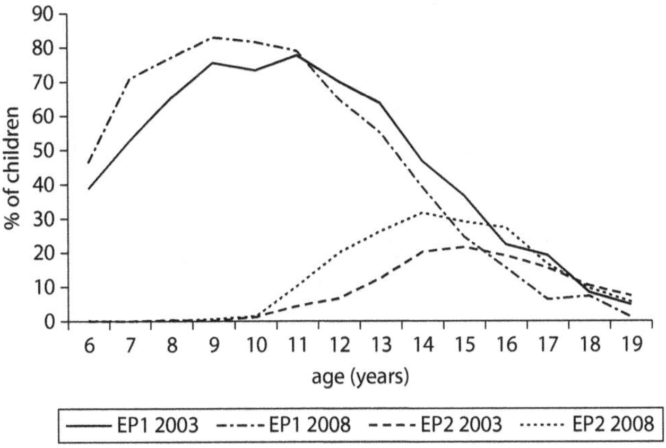

*Sources:* MICS 2008, IAF 2002–03.

**Table 3.3 Time to Complete a Grade-Level Cycle by Age, 2008**

| Grade level | Age | | Time (years) to complete level | |
|---|---|---|---|---|
| | Official | Observed (average) | Official | Observed |
| Start 1st grade | 6 | 9 | | |
| Finish 5th grade | 11 | 14 | 5 | 6 |
| Finish 7th grade | 13 | 16 | 2 | 2 |
| Finish 10th grade | 16 | 19 | 3 | 3 |

*Source:* NPS 2008.
*Note:* These figures are calculated using only people who were shown in the data as starting 1st grade. Individuals who started 1st grade before 1998 are not included in this calculation. Age is observed for last occurrence of grades 5, 7, and 10 (for people repeating, only the last, successful instance is counted). Sample size is small (120 observations) for 10th grade, so these results must be taken with caution. Sample size for 12th grade (completion of ES2) is below 20 observations, so these results are not reported.

level, the average age of entry into 1st grade is 9 years.[4] Despite entering school over three years later than the official age, these children have more or less progressed smoothly through the system, although there is a considerable loss of efficiency in lower primary. On average, one full year was lost through repetition, even for children who completed 5th grade. This represents a significant fiscal cost to Mozambique. The reasons for the high repetition of 5th grade should be explored in more detail.

Note that the figures in table 3.3 include only children who completed the corresponding level (grades 5, 7, and 10). Therefore, they are not representative of all children enrolling in school. Repetition rates, in fact, are higher for the student population as a whole, as can be seen in table 3.4. Nevertheless, it is interesting to note that for these children, late entry does not appear to be related to higher dropout or repetition rates (beyond lower primary). This suggests that for these children, the consequences of late entry into schooling might be felt later in life in terms of opportunity costs and loss in lifetime earnings.

Table 3.4 shows high average repetition rates in lower and upper primary for the student population as a whole, particularly in grades 5, 7, and 8. High repetition in these grades could be a cause for failure to complete the level.

Table 3.4 also shows that grade repetition has decreased significantly since 2004 for grades 3 and 4. This is likely to be a result of semi-automatic promotion, introduced with the primary reforms in that year. However, repetition rates in grade 5 have increased slightly, suggesting that more students are being held back before completing the lower primary level. Since most children who were in grade 7 and beyond in 2007 were not likely to have benefited from the 2004 semi-automatic promotion instituted in lower primary reforms, it remains to be seen how this will affect repetition rates at the higher levels.

In 2003 there were fewer children age 15 out of school, probably reflecting that children entered later. Although in 2008 there were fewer younger children who were not attending school (see figure 3.7), by age 15 close to 50 percent of youngsters in Mozambique are out of school. This indicates not only the challenges for human capital formation but also the likely persistence of a poorly educated labor force, which will hamper growth.

## Vulnerable Groups: Orphans

> *There are now more orphans in school than before, but their overall educational attainment is still lower than for non-orphans.*

Orphans are one of the most vulnerable groups of children in Mozambique.[5] Estimates of the orphan population are 12–16 percent of the child population (between 1.2 and 1.6 million children were orphaned in 2006, according to UNICEF). Orphans in Mozambique are more likely to live in households where the head has no education. While all children are regularly asked to take part in domestic activities and chores, orphans are

**Table 3.4  Repetition Rates by Grade and Year, 1998–2007**

| | Grade | | | | | | | | | | | |
|---|---|---|---|---|---|---|---|---|---|---|---|---|
| Year | 1 | 2 | 3 | 4 | 5 | 6 | 7 | 8 | 9 | 10 | 11 | 12 | Average |
| 1998 | 18.6 | 4.1 | 9.9 | 6.0 | 14.1 | 15.6 | 10.9 | 2.6 | 26.0 | 0.0 | 0.0 | n.a. | 11.7 |
| 1999 | 8.2 | 15.9 | 12.7 | 9.5 | 5.7 | 14.7 | 21.2 | 11.8 | 17.9 | 0.0 | 0.0 | 0.0 | 11.5 |
| 2000 | 7.6 | 15.6 | 14.3 | 16.8 | 15.2 | 21.1 | 15.2 | 8.1 | 3.2 | 0.0 | 0.0 | n.a. | 13.4 |
| 2001 | 16.1 | 10.6 | 18.4 | 9.2 | 23.1 | 16.0 | 13.5 | 12.5 | 18.7 | 33.2 | 0.0 | n.a. | 15.0 |
| 2002 | 8.4 | 16.9 | 10.9 | 11.0 | 16.3 | 10.5 | 19.3 | 29.8 | 23.7 | 17.2 | 18.5 | 73.9 | 12.9 |
| **2003** | **14.6** | **14.0** | **12.3** | **12.3** | **18.1** | **7.6** | **22.8** | **24.8** | **11.0** | **33.2** | **0.0** | **0.0** | **14.3** |
| 2004 | 8.0 | 14.9 | 12.8 | 17.0 | 22.0 | 11.7 | 15.4 | 25.2 | 21.7 | 30.4 | 0.0 | 9.1 | 14.5 |
| 2005 | 9.2 | 15.1 | 12.2 | 7.8 | 19.3 | 8.5 | 17.0 | 19.0 | 7.8 | 36.4 | 5.7 | 25.7 | 12.8 |
| 2006 | 16.9 | 17.0 | 11.6 | 9.6 | 10.6 | 2.8 | 16.9 | 19.6 | 18.8 | 27.8 | 11.7 | 23.5 | 13.8 |
| **2007** | **13.7** | **10.4** | **6.9** | **6.4** | **20.0** | **2.0** | **5.4** | **13.7** | **11.3** | **23.0** | **3.1** | **19.1** | **10.4** |
| Average | 12.3 | 13.9 | 11.8 | 10.2 | 17.1 | 7.9 | 14.8 | 18.6 | 14.7 | 26.5 | 5.0 | 20.4 | 13.0 |

*Sources:* NPS 2008, Education History Module.

*Note:* Sample sizes are small (<100 observed) beginning in 9th grade. These are calculated for any student who was in school for two consecutive years and was in the same grade in both years. n.a. = not available.

**Figure 3.7  Children Not Attending School, by Age, 2003 and 2008**

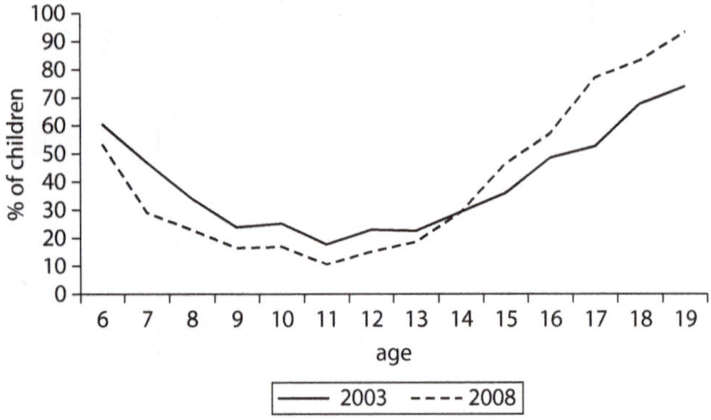

*Sources:* MICS 2008, IAF 2002–03.

substantially more likely to spend time on chores than non-orphans, both in urban and rural areas (Fox et al. 2008).

In general, Mozambican orphans are less likely to be enrolled in school. In 2003, 75 percent of poor orphans of school age in urban areas attended school, compared to 96 percent of non-poor orphans and 95 percent of poor non-orphans. In rural areas the number of poor orphans not attending school is just as high, but because attendance by all children in rural areas is lower, the difference is less striking (Fox et al. 2008).

A comparison of 2003 and 2008 data suggests that even though the ratio of orphans to non-orphans attending school remains below unity, orphans' attendance rate has seen some improvement in recent years, particularly for maternal and "double" orphans (that is, children without both mother and father) (see table 3.5).

The gap between orphans and non-orphans seems to have been improving since as early as 2003. Nationally representative data from 1997 and 2003 Demographic and Health Surveys show the difference in school attendance declining between orphans and non-orphans, with the gap closing more for male than for female orphans (Fox et al. 2008).

In terms of dropout rates, data from 2008 reveal that orphans, particularly maternal and double-orphans, left school at much higher rates than non-orphans (see figure 3.8).

Financial reasons are probably the main reason for orphans to not enroll in school or to drop out, especially for the higher grades (Valerio et al. 2006; Fox et al. 2008). Other factors, however, are also responsible. Case, Paxson, and Ableidinger (2004) found that children in Africa

**Table 3.5 Ratio of Current School Attendance of Orphans vs. Non-Orphans, 2003 and 2008**

| Type of orphan | 2003 | 2008 |
| --- | --- | --- |
| Maternal | 0.81 | 0.94 |
| Paternal | 0.97 | 0.98 |
| Both parents died | 0.80 | 0.93 |

*Sources:* For 2003 data, Fox et al. 2008, using Government of Mozambique 2006 data (based on Demographic and Health Survey data). For 2008 data, MICS 2008. All estimates are weighted.
*Note:* Estimates are for children age 18 and younger.

**Figure 3.8 Dropout Rates by Education Level and Type of Orphan, 2008**

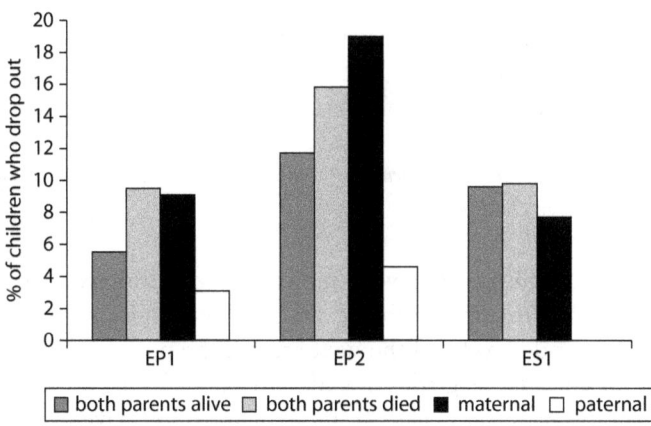

*Source:* MICS 2008.
*Note:* These rates are calculated as the proportion of people in that year who responded "drop out" to the question of "at the end of the school year did the student...."

without mothers or fathers or who live with family members other than their parents are less likely to enroll in school, not only because of poverty but also because of discrimination against household members who are not biologically related.

## Completion Rates

> *Most children who enter lower primary do not complete this level when they should.*

Despite significant improvements in enrollment rates and other educational indicators, completion rates for primary school remain extremely low. (Completion is measured by the highest educational level attained for the population that ever attended school.) Only about 10 percent (rural) to 20 percent (urban) of the students finish EP1 at the official age of 10 (see figure 3.9).

Data presented in figure 3.9 show that average completion rates are delayed by approximately two years for urban students and by four years for rural students (beyond the official completion age). This is to be expected given the large number of late school entrants and grade repeaters. However, the rate only reaches close to 100 percent at ages 18–19 for urban children, while it remains well below 60 percent for rural children, even at older ages. This suggests most children in rural areas never actually complete lower primary.

At the upper primary school level, completion rates are low over all ages 12–19 (see figure 3.10). The highest rates of completion are 50 percent, for urban children, but are negligible in rural areas, where most children live.

> *The transition to upper primary remains an elusive goal for most Mozambican children.*

Even among those who have completed lower primary, a large share does not go on to upper primary. Smooth age-appropriate transitions between one grade level and the next are not the norm. Table 3.6 shows "smooth" or continuous grade-to-grade transitions.[6] Out of 100 children who began lower primary in 1998, 66 percent would have made it up to

**Figure 3.9 Lower Primary School Completion Rate, 2008**

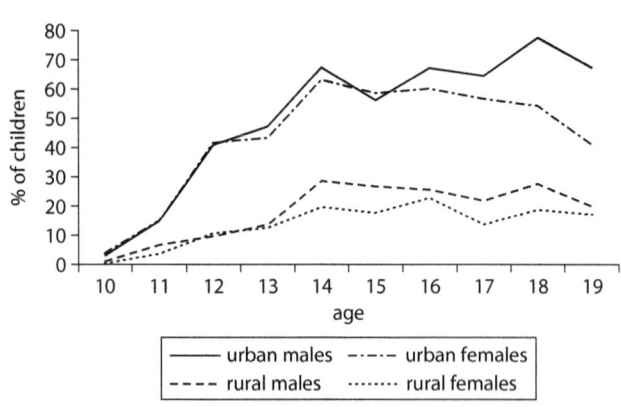

*Source:* MICS 2008.
*Note:* The completion rate is defined as the percentage of students with the highest level of education (EP1 or higher) over the population of age 10 (the official EP1 completion age).

**Figure 3.10 Upper Primary School Completion Rate, 2008**

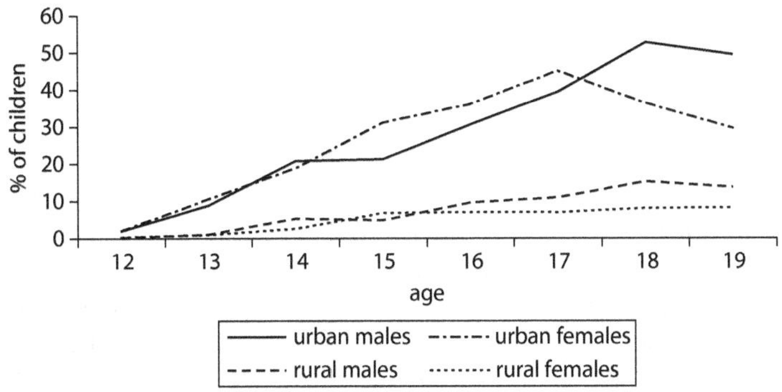

*Source:* MICS 2008.
*Note:* The completion rate is defined as the percentage of students with the highest level of education (EP2 or higher) over the population of age 12 (the official EP2 completion age).

**Table 3.6 Student Survival (in number of students) by Year of Entry into 1st Grade**

| Grade | 1998 | 1999 | 2000 | 2001 | 2002 | 2003 | 2004 | 2005 | 2006 | 2007 |
|---|---|---|---|---|---|---|---|---|---|---|
| 1 | 100 | 100 | 100 | 100 | 100 | 100 | 100 | 100 | 100 | 100 |
| 2 | 81 | 91 | 89 | 83 | 91 | 83 | 89 | 88 | 78 | 79 |
| 3 | 66 | 73 | 79 | 64 | 75 | 68 | 73 | 67 | 66 | |
| 4 | 52 | 52 | 67 | 53 | 63 | 57 | 61 | 57 | | |
| 5 | 48 | 42 | 56 | 42 | 57 | 48 | 54 | | | |
| 6 | 37 | 35 | 40 | 33 | 43 | 36 | | | | |
| 7 | 30 | 29 | 30 | 25 | 36 | | | | | |
| 8 | 21 | 21 | 19 | 13 | | | | | | |
| 9 | 15 | 14 | 15 | | | | | | | |
| 10 | 8 | 11 | | | | | | | | |
| 11 | 5 | | | | | | | | | |
| Baseline N | 275 | 260 | 278 | 325 | 359 | 361 | 433 | 432 | 454 | 515 |

*Source:* NPS 2008.
*Note:* The year columns refer to the year the person began 1st grade. Assuming 100 people begin the 1st grade, the next row represents how many of those survived to the 2nd grade and so forth (based on grade-to-grade transition rates for that cohort).

3rd grade, 48 percent to 5th grade, and 37 percent to 6th grade (upper primary). Only 30 percent would have completed upper primary (grade 7). In 2002, 36 percent of students who began 6 years earlier were reaching grade 7.[7]

In the key transition point between lower primary and upper primary (5th to 6th grade) a similar proportion of students dropped out between 1998 and 2003. Only between a quarter and a third were making it to the last grade of upper primary (grade 7). This proportion, however, was higher in 2002 than in 1998, suggesting improvement in completion rates in lower primary and absorption into upper primary. It should be noted that because the NPS Education History Module only collected information up to 2008, it is not yet possible to observe year-to-year transitions for a full cohort that began primary school after the 2004–05 reforms. The cohort of students who began 1$^{st}$ grade in 2004 are only observed when they reach 5$^{th}$ grade in 2008. Future analyses should investigate transitions further to observe whether any significant trends emerge.

The system's lack of adequate grade-to-grade progression and completion could be a result of demand-side (cost, parental preferences, cultural issues) or supply-side barriers (lack of schools, lack of qualified teachers, poor quality of schooling). Poor households in rural areas probably are most likely to suffer from both demand-side and supply side-constraints. Poor households in urban areas probably are affected more by demand issues than by supply issues; however, these barriers affect all Mozambicans to some degree.

> *It is likely that significant demand-side barriers remain, particularly in upper primary.*

While the 2004–05 reforms abolished official school fees, other direct and indirect costs (uniforms, transportation, school lunch, opportunity [labor] cost) remain important limitations to schooling, particularly at the upper primary level. A considerable proportion of households in Mozambique continue to pay obligatory and voluntary fees in lower and upper primary, even though school fees were legally abolished in the country. NPS data show that 52.4 percent of households report having paid an obligatory contribution to their child's EP1 school in 2007 (see table 3.7). In the poorest consumption quintile households, this proportion was 36 percent.

Focus groups conducted by the World Bank in 2007 showed that with the onset of the reforms, rural schools lost income from school fees. Therefore, for many schools, voluntary parent contributions became the only source of income in addition to ADE income, which was perceived by some actors to be insufficient (World Bank 2007).

Particularly in the southern part of the country, informants said that voluntary contributions were perceived to be "obligatory" and there was added pressure from the community to comply (World Bank 2007).

Furthermore, other direct school costs (school materials, uniforms, snacks, etc.) also remain a significant source of household expenditures. The World

**Table 3.7 Households with Positive Education Expenditures (cash and in-kind) by Per Capita Consumption Quintile, 2008**

| Education expenditures | Households with children ages 6–17 attending EP1 (% households in quintile) | | | | | | Households with children ages 12–19 attending EP2 (% households in quintile) | | | | | |
|---|---|---|---|---|---|---|---|---|---|---|---|---|
| | 1 | 2 | 3 | 4 | 5 | Avg | 1 | 2 | 3 | 4 | 5 | Avg |
| Payment to the school (obligatory) | 36 | 49 | 39 | 70 | 67 | 52 | 57 | 68 | 57 | 77 | 84 | 69 |
| Payment to the school (voluntary) | 21 | 31 | 46 | 54 | 76 | 46 | 25 | 43 | 62 | 62 | 82 | 55 |
| Material | 75 | 81 | 88 | 88 | 88 | 84 | 85 | 91 | 96 | 95 | 98 | 93 |
| Other expenditures | 9 | 14 | 19 | 40 | 52 | 27 | 11 | 16 | 33 | 45 | 68 | 34 |

*Source:* NPS 2008.

Bank (2007) focus groups revealed that school materials, mainly school uniforms, are the most relevant expenditure for households. And NPS data show that school materials (including uniforms) are the most significant share of total household expenditures on primary education.

According to participants in the focus groups, the cost of uniforms is felt more acutely in rural areas, where parents cannot afford to provide ordinary clothing for their children much less a uniform that costs 150–250 Mt per child. Parents in rural areas mentioned that although the uniform was not mandatory, their children "cry at home" when they do not have it and feel "ashamed" (World Bank 2007).

The "Direct Support to Schools" program (ADE) was designed to alleviate parental expenditures on consumable school materials, such as notebooks or pencils. However, participants in the focus groups mentioned that children only receive one notebook and one pencil through ADE. Because this is not enough to last throughout the year, they need to pay for additional material (World Bank 2007).

> *Other reasons, in addition to financial ones, also impede children from starting school on time and successfully finishing lower and upper primary.*

Analysis of the study conducted for this report does not allow a definitive conclusion on whether current costs constitute actual barriers to school entry and permanence. There is some indication, however, that financial considerations are not the main reason why parents keep their children, particularly young children, out of school. According to NPS data, parental perception of "not being of school age" is the top reason why parents have not enrolled their children in school (see figure 3.11).

Poor indicators for early childhood development (that is, stunting, low birth weight, delayed language development) could help explain why parents perceive that many young children of the official school age are not ready for school. Studies in other countries, such as Ghana (Glewwe and Jacoby 1995), show that nutritional deficiencies can be responsible for children starting school late. And if indeed the children are not ready for school, this may partially explain high repetition and dropout rates.

## Secondary Education

The previous chapter shows that since 2000, and certainly after the 2004 reforms, primary school enrollment has been rising in Mozambique. In addition, more children were starting school earlier and staying in school slightly longer. A program of school construction in lower and upper primary also appears to have contributed to removing some of the supply-side constraints preventing children from enrolling in primary school. These factors in primary are likely to have affected secondary schooling. This chapter reviews enrollment and other indicators at the secondary level using descriptive evidence from surveys and other data.

**Figure 3.11 Reasons for Not Enrolling Children in School by Age, 1998–2008**

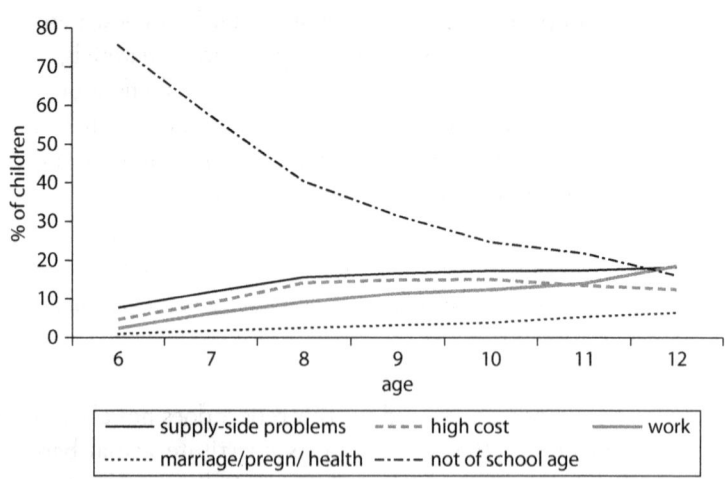

*Source:* NPS 2008, Education History Module.
*Note:* The percentage reflects the average share at each age of people mentioning that reason for their children not attending school over the period 1998–2008.

## Analysis of the Effects of the 2004–05 Reforms: Outputs and Outcomes

> *Increased access and permanence in primary school also put pressure on secondary schools.*

One of the most important indirect effects of the primary school reforms—motivating students to enroll and remain longer in school—is likely to have caused the secondary school enrollment increase that Mozambique experienced after 2004. This increase was likely fueled not only by the demand induced by the abolition of fees in primary, but also by the Mozambique Government's effort to build more secondary schools and improve access in previously underserved areas. As primary school GERs increased between 1997 and 2008, so too did GERs in secondary schools grow significantly, particularly in lower secondary (see figure 3.12).

Although gross enrollment grew across the board, rural areas saw spectacular growth between 1997 and 2010, from rates as low as 1.2 percent for females and 3.5 percent for males, to close to 25 percent for rural men and 16 percent for rural women. Enrollment of males in urban areas also grew considerably, from 27 percent in 1997 to close to 87 percent in 2008. In upper secondary, although GERs are low in general, they experienced rapid growth in this time period, particularly for rural males.

Between 2000 and 2003 the numbers of schools grew by more than 30 percent for lower secondary schools and by more than 45 percent for upper secondary schools. And after 2004 the number of lower secondary

**Figure 3.12 Gross Enrollment Rates in Secondary Schools, 1997, 2003, and 2008**

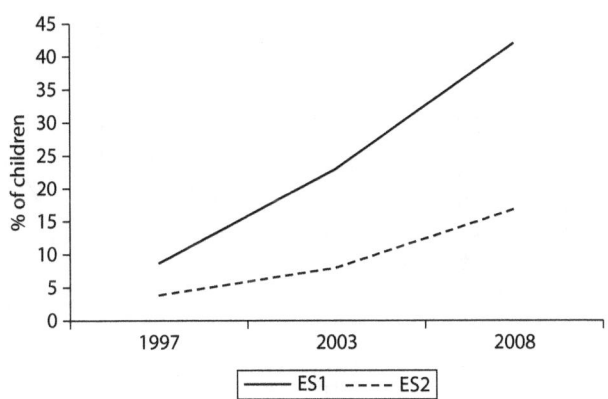

*Sources:* MICS 2008, IAF 2002-03, IAF 1996-97.
*Note:* This table uses the age groups prior to the 2006 change: ages 14–16 in ES1 and 17–18 in ES2.

schools more than doubled and upper secondary tripled. From 2004 to 2010 the number of teachers in lower secondary schools also more than doubled (MEC 2010); figures are not available for upper secondary.

> *Serious supply constraints persist despite a large expansion in the network of secondary schools.*

The growth in the number of schools seems very large because the country had so few schools in 2000: fewer than 100 lower secondary schools and only 20 upper secondary schools. Even in 2009, after spectacular growth, there were fewer than 400 lower secondary schools and around 120 upper secondary schools in the country. Secondary school access is still unevenly distributed among the provinces: Cabo Delgado has fewer than 10 upper secondary schools and Niassa and Tete have even fewer (see figure 3.13).

Thus, even after the two- or three-fold increase in the number of secondary schools, the supply is still not enough to meet demand. Interviews with parents, teachers, and school officials reveal a widespread perception that lack of sufficient places in secondary schools was the main barrier to access at this level (World Bank 2007).

Because rural areas are particularly underserved, rural students must travel long distances to the nearest secondary school and often need to

**Figure 3.13  Number of Secondary Schools by Province, 2009**

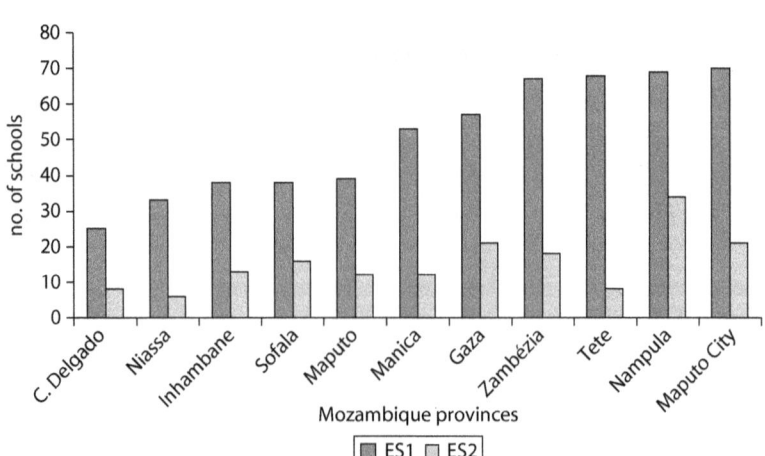

*Source:* MEC 2009.

board there. But few schools have boarding facilities, thus preventing many students from enrolling for lack of a place to stay.

Although lack of school spots was perceived to be more acute for rural students, a good number of urban students face the same challenge even though their parents can afford matriculation fees and other direct costs (World Bank 2007). The lack of places appeared to be more significant for those entering 8$^{th}$ grade and those in transit from 10$^{th}$ to 11$^{th}$ grade. Thus it appears that the supply side is the binding constraint in most regions of the country.

> *The rapid growth in the private secondary school sector suggests that supply-side constraints are a key barrier to access.*

To determine how binding supply constraints are on access, public school growth can be compared to the growth in the private school sector. Figure 3.14 shows that the percentage of enrollment in public schools is considerably lower for secondary schools.

Ministry of Education census data for the 2004 and 2009 school years, shown in figure 3.15, suggest that although growth in the number of

**Figure 3.14 Enrollment in Public Schools as a Percentage of Total Enrollment, 2009**

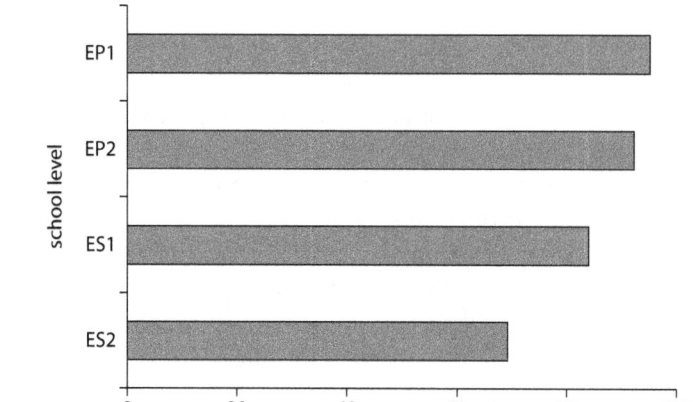

*Source:* MEC census data 2009; MEC 2010.
*Note:* This is calculated as the percentage of enrollment in day and night shifts in public schools, over total enrollment.

**Figure 3.15 Growth in Public and Private Secondary Schools between 2004 and 2009**

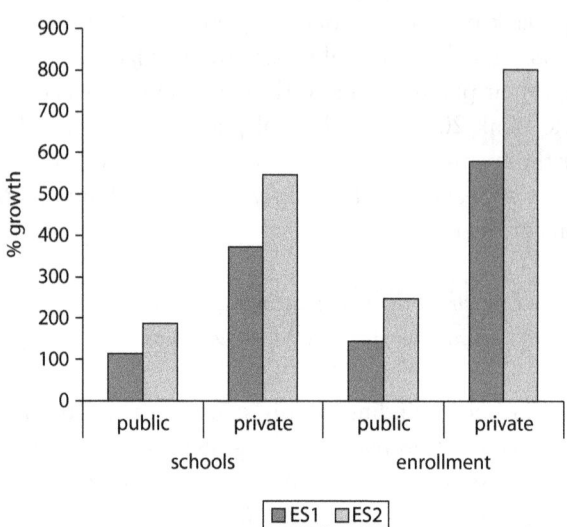

Sources: MEC 2005; MEC 2009, 13–14, 43–49.
Note: Includes day and night shifts.

schools and enrollment in the public sector has been considerable, it has been even larger in the private sector.

## Private Sector Education Is Growing

Clearly, many students and families in Mozambique are willing to pay to attend secondary school. Moreover, these families may also be paying a premium to access better quality secondary schools.

NPS does not have data on whether an individual attended a public or a private school. However, some data on obligatory contributions (fees) to schools might illustrate the fact that higher socioeconomic status families spend more money on education and presumably (although the data are not conclusive on this point) on private schooling. For example, 70 percent of quintile 4 and 5 households pay obligatory contributions in EP1 vs. 40 percent of quintile 1 households. In upper primary, 80 percent of quintile 4 and 5 pay obligatory contributions vs. 60 percent of quintile 1 households. And the size of the contribution is much higher in the higher SES households: 50 Mt for quintile 5 vs. 5 Mt for quintile 1 in lower primary.

Overall, focus groups and other respondents interviewed for the World Bank study perceived private secondary schools as being of much higher quality than public secondary schools. Most respondents from private schools indicated that their schools had libraries with sufficient books and that teachers had books and other teaching materials. These schools also had more availability of computers and Internet access than public schools.

## Quality at Issue

Supply constraints, therefore, not only point to a shortage of secondary schools in the country, but also to a shortage of *quality* secondary schooling. This apparently drives many better-off families, particularly in urban areas, to the private sector.

> *Pressures on the limited network of public secondary schools and the amount of resources needed at this level has affected quality.*

Growth in enrollment puts enormous pressure on public secondary schools. Contrary to the case of private schools, where parents perceived physical and learning conditions to be adequate, the quality of public secondary schools is perceived to be low (World Bank 2007). This is further complicated by the sheer amount of resources needed to build a high-quality secondary school infrastructure. Learning at this level requires teachers trained in the specific subjects (mathematics, science, and so forth), specialized learning materials (a greater number of textbooks, pedagogical aides, and so forth), and often well-equipped libraries, computer access, and laboratories.

The physical conditions of secondary schools, however, were perceived by many respondents to be extremely poor: lack of classrooms, lack of furniture, poor or nonexistent bathroom facilities, lack of basic maintenance and upkeep, among others. In addition, most secondary schools lack functioning libraries, laboratories, and computers and Internet access.

Class size in public lower secondary is more than 60 students and has grown substantially since 2004. Class size in all of the schools visited for the qualitative study had expanded considerably. The average classroom in a secondary school in Nampula, for example, contained more than 120 students.

The poor working conditions that teachers face (low salaries, long working hours, lack of monitoring and support) do not help to recruit and retain the best individuals as teachers. Parents and students complained of some teachers "without the right qualifications and who lack motivation and professional attitude" (World Bank 2007).

Moreover, there appears to be a significant lack of female teachers at both levels of secondary education. A better balance in the number of female and male teachers would contribute to a school environment more supportive of girls and alleviate the problem of sexual harassment of female students by male teachers that has been reported (World Bank 2007).

> *Considerable demand-side barriers to accessing the secondary level still exist, cost being an important issue for many families.*

Considerable demand-side barriers to secondary schooling exist in Mozambique, and these are felt more acutely in rural areas and districts. Respondents consistently mentioned direct (fees, books, and so on) and indirect (opportunity) costs of schooling as key barriers to access in both public and private sectors (World Bank 2007).

Results from the NPS suggest that economic reasons, such as the child having to work or not being able to afford books or school fees, led as many as half of the students to drop out of secondary school. Although these results are tentative due to small sample sizes, they suggest that economic reasons are a significant explanation for the lack of effective completion rates at the secondary level.

The fact that many students are not able to afford books at the secondary level was also echoed in interviews and focus groups. Interviewees stated that because books for this level were expensive, many students and even teachers did not have the textbooks for either classroom or home study. The fact that many schools do not have functioning libraries adds to an already dire situation in this regard.

Other sociocultural and economic factors reported by interview respondents and focus groups that affect secondary school enrollment and permanence include early pregnancy and marriage (for girls) and migration to South Africa (affecting mostly boys) (World Bank 2007).

The low perceived quality in most secondary schools in the public sector, as well as the high fees charged, might also have contributed to lower demand among lower income families for secondary schooling. Thus, demand-side barriers clearly keep lower income households and parents of girls from even trying to compete for the few quality secondary school places available.

*The pressure on secondary schools is only likely to get worse.*

The 2004-05 primary school reforms appear to have motivated more children to enroll in and complete primary school. Their success has encouraged more children to want to advance on to secondary school. The physical and pedagogical conditions of secondary schooling, as well as ensuring adequate access in rural areas and for girls, will become even more pressing issues in the years to come.

It is difficult from these data to determine whether the increase in secondary school enrollment was caused by the demand aspect of the primary reforms (by reducing the cost of staying in primary, more students stayed and progressed on to secondary), or by the expansion of secondary schools, which made this level accessible to areas previously underserved.

The econometric analysis in the next chapter suggests that much of the enrollment in secondary school was probably fueled by higher enrollment and permanence in primary school after the 2004–05 reforms. Nonetheless, because of the spectacular growth in secondary supply after 2004, it is difficult to distinguish the effect of secondary school expansion from that of the 2004–05 primary reforms.

## Notes

1. Official enrollment ages in Mozambique for primary and secondary schools changed in 2006. Before 2006, the official age for lower primary (EP1) was 6–11 and for upper primary (EP2) it was 12–13. In lower secondary (ES1) it was 14–16 and for upper secondary (ES2) it was 17–18. After 2006 the official enrollment ages are 6–10 (EP1), 11–12 (EP2), 13–15 (ES1), and 16–17 (ES2). For consistency, this report uses the "old" official ages for all GER and NER calculations.
2. Smaller sample sizes for children in EP2 may be partly responsible for the jump in reported fees in the middle of the distribution.
3. We thank one of our reviewers for pointing this out.
4. These data come from NPS and are thus not representative of the whole country (as IAF or MICS are), although the level of precision in the estimates is adequate. However, this analysis needed the panel aspect of NPS to be able to track children who began in $1^{st}$ grade and follow them through $5^{th}$ grade and beyond.
5. In Mozambique the word "orphan" is usually used to refer to a child who has lost one or both parents. Maternal orphans are those whose mother has died.

Paternal orphans are those whose father has died. Double orphans are children who have lost both parents.

6. These represent survival rates for the same cohort of students who began 1st grade in the corresponding year. Two caveats: first, because sample sizes are small in some of these calculations, estimates should be taken with caution. And second, most of the repetition and dropouts happen in the later primary grades. A longer panel might be able to uncover a different pattern in grades 5 and 7.

7. The Education History Module in the NPS (2008) is not long enough to show how smooth transition rates have changed for cohorts that began after the 2004–05 reforms.

## References

Case, A., C. Paxson, and J. Ableidinger. 2004. "Orphans in Africa: Parental Death, Poverty, and School Enrollment." *Demography* 41 (3): 483–508.

Fox, L., R. M. Benfica, M. Ehrenpreis, M. S. Gaal, H. Nordang, and D. Owen. 2008. *Beating the Odds: Sustaining Inclusion in a Growing Economy: A Mozambique Poverty, Gender, and Social Assessment.* Washington, DC: World Bank.

Glewwe, P., and H. G. Jacoby. 1995. "An Economic Analysis of Delayed Primary School Enrollment in a Low-Income Country: The Role of Early Childhood Nutrition." *The Review of Economics and Statistics* 77 (1): 156–69.

MEC (Ministério da Educação e Cultura). 2005. "Levantamiento Estatístico 03 Marco." Database, Government of Mozambique, Maputo, Mozambique.

———. 2009. "Estatística da Educação. Levantamento Escolar 2009." Government of Mozambique, Maputo, Mozambique.

———. 2010. "Os resultados do sector através dos principais indicadores." (Progress Report). Ministry of Education and Culture, Government of Mozambique, Maputo, Mozambique.

Valerio, A., E. Bardasi, A. Chambal, and M. F. Lobo. 2006. "Mozambique: School Fees and Primary School Enrollment Retention." In *Poverty and Social Impact Analysis of Reforms: Lessons and Examples from Implementation*, 93–148, ed. A. Coudouel, A. A. Dani, and S. Paternostro. Washington, DC: World Bank.

Wils, A. 2004. "Late Entrants Leave School Early: Evidence from Mozambique." *International Review of Education* 50 (1): 17–37.

World Bank. 2005. "Poverty and Social Impact Analysis: Primary School Enrollment and Retention—The Impact of School Fees." World Bank, Washington, DC.

———. 2007. "PSIA II—Follow-up Study of Primary Education and Baseline Study of Secondary Education, Mozambique." World Bank, Washington, DC.

CHAPTER 4

# The Effects of the Primary Reforms: Econometric Analysis

As the analysis has shown, after the 2004–05 reforms, enrollment in lower and upper primary surged, and, while financial and other barriers remained (especially in upper primary), overall direct costs of education decreased. But that analysis is merely descriptive and does not lead to the conclusion that the changes in enrollment were due to the reforms or that the slowdown in the rate of change in enrollment after 2004 would have been even slower in the absence of the reforms (see box 4.1).

To address the question of whether the change in enrollment observed can be partially attributed to the reforms of 2004–05 with a more robust methodology, an econometric analysis was carried out taking advantage of the Education History Module of the NPS 2008 data and its ability to track individual schooling decisions over time, and most importantly for purposes of evaluation, before and after the reforms. The technical description of the model and results of this analysis can be found in appendix C.

The analysis was performed using the Education History Module of NPS to obtain information regarding enrollment status and level attended for each individual for each year between 1998 and 2008. Models predicting enrollment were estimated for the whole population ages 6–18 and separately for urban, rural, males, and females. Enrollment before and after the 2004–05 reforms was predicted. This approach follows the

> **Box 4.1**
>
> ## Difficulties of Assessing Reform Impact
>
> Much of social science and public policy research deals with a fundamental problem in evaluation: how to attribute a particular outcome to a public policy when it is impossible to observe the program participant (beneficiary) in the alternate, counterfactual state of no treatment. In other words, how can we know that a certain outcome was in fact *caused* by a policy or program rather than other factors? Other factors that could also affect the intended outcome are (1) other public programs in place and (2) increased income or other changes in the household that might have affected demand for education (the outcome).
>
> Such difficulties exist when evaluating the impact of the primary reforms in Mozambique. Primary school enrollment had been increasing since at least 1997, and probably even before (World Bank 2005), so if a higher primary enrollment rate is also observed from 2003 to 2008, can it be attributed to the primary reforms or simply be a continuation of the previous trend, which itself may have been caused by other factors, such as increased household income resulting from economic development?
>
> Conducting randomized trials or generating natural experiments would provide an adequate counterfactual, but this is difficult, so researchers usually conduct quasi-experimental research and take advantage of particularly rich datasets to generate an adequate method of identifying program impact. The success of these methods depends on how robust the counterfactual is that is developed by the researcher from the data. Nevertheless, it is important to keep in mind the old saying in statistics and social science: correlation does not imply causation.
>
> *Source:* Authors.

method of Duflo (2001) using time (year) and child's age to identify the effect of the program (see appendix C).

The econometric results strongly indicate that the 2004–05 reforms were an important factor in the increased enrollment observed, that is, owing to the reforms, primary education enrollment grew even faster than they otherwise would have. The effects were experienced across all school age groups. After the 2004–05 reforms were implemented, the probability of enrolling in school increased for all individuals ages 6–18, controlling for all other variables measured in the survey, which are expected to affect the probability of enrollment (that is, household demand for education). The reforms also appear to have increased enrollment in secondary schools because of higher enrollment and completion rates in lower primary.

Figure 4.1 shows the estimated probability of enrollment by age before and after the program, based on the econometric model (that is, controlling for all other variables known to affect enrollment). The upward shift in enrollment for all ages observed after the 2004–05 reforms (that is, after the program) shows the estimated program effects. The hump in the curve around ages 6–12 (the main ages for EP1), with a peak occurring at age 9 and a decline thereafter, indicates that the effect was strongest at the peak age for enrollment in EP1. At age 13, the program variable has an insignificant coefficient. This may indicate that the program effect on demand for EP2 was limited by the higher cost and lower supply of schools. On average, the reforms led to a 12 percent increase in the probability of attending school for children ages 6–18.

It is difficult to ascertain whether all of the enrollment growth was due to the 2004–05 reforms. Some increase might be due to the increased supply of schools, as most of the new lower primary schools built between 1996 and 2005 were in rural areas. The analysis suggests, however, that a

**Figure 4.1 Marginal Effect on Enrollment Before and After the Program, by Age Group, 6–18 Years**

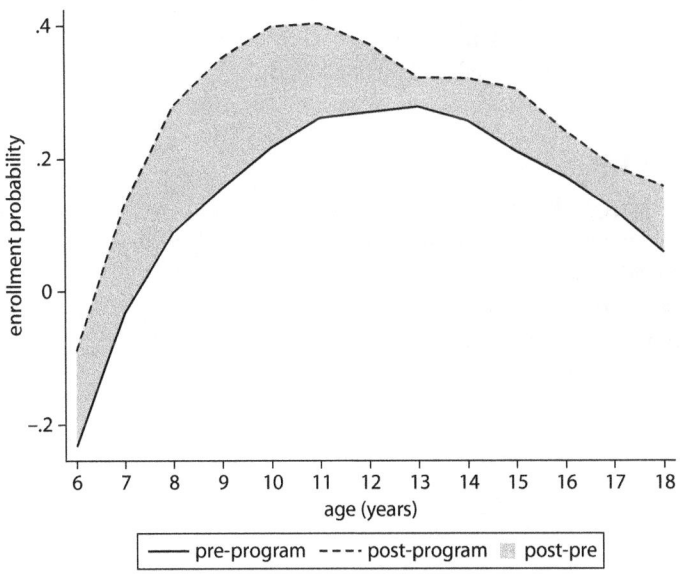

*Note:* See Appendix C for derivation.

significant proportion of children were enrolled or remained in lower and upper primary school after 2005, probably as a consequence of the reforms.

> *The program improved access for Mozambique's most disadvantaged groups, but significant biases against girls and orphans remain.*

The results also show that the 2004–05 reforms benefitted Mozambique's most disadvantaged groups: girls and children in rural areas, but only with respect to EP1. Primary education enrollment was estimated to have grown even faster than it otherwise would have in these groups. Enrollment gains in EP1 were highest among poor households. In EP2, more children enrolled across all sectors of the population, but gains were highest for the better-off households.

However, the analysis confirms that significant biases against orphans' access to education still exist. Despite improved enrollment for all age groups in Mozambique after the 2004–05 reforms (including orphans), orphans are still less likely to be enrolled, especially when the mother is missing. When the mother has died, both boys and girls suffer a lower probability of enrollment, but the effect is worse for girls. Interestingly, when the father has died, the probability of enrollment only worsens for girls. The analysis also finds that the probability of lower enrollment for children whose mother has died is higher in rural areas than in urban areas. There is no significant effect on enrollment by area of residence for children whose father has died.

## References

Duflo, E. 2001. "Schooling and Labor Market Consequences of School Construction in Indonesia: Evidence from an Unusual Policy Experiment." *The American Economic Review* 91 (4): 795–813.

World Bank. 2005. "Poverty and Social Impact Analysis: Primary School Enrollment and Retention—The Impact of School Fees." World Bank, Washington, DC.

CHAPTER 5

# Does Education Matter for Poverty Reduction? A Livelihoods Perspective

Expanding access to education[1] has been a key policy goal for Mozambique, not only as an end in itself, but also because the lack of a qualified labor force is a constraint to growth and poverty reduction.[2] This discussion has gained relevance because recent data suggest that Mozambique's growth has not reduced poverty to the extent it did in the past decade (MPD 2010). Questions have been raised about the role of education and skills in supporting an inclusive pattern of employment expansion and changing the growth trajectory toward creating increased opportunities for all households.

Growth improves the welfare of households primarily by allowing the labor force to move from lower productivity into higher productivity activities. In 2008, 88 percent of primary employment was found in household-based activities—either farming or non-farm enterprises. The majority of those employed in the household sector reported that their primary activity was agriculture (see table 5.1). This situation is expected to change quite slowly over the next decade.

***Demand for labor was low in the past.*** Relative to the size of the labor force, few enterprises in Mozambique, large or small, offer wage and salary employment. In 2008 only 7.8 percent of the labor force reported private-sector, non-agricultural, wage and salary employment as their primary

**Table 5.1  Structure of Employment, Household vs. Wage, 1997–2009**

| Type of employment | Share of employment (%) | | |
|---|---|---|---|
| | 1997 | 2003 | 2009 |
| Household agriculture | 86.8 | 80.1 | 79.6 |
| Non-farm household enterprise | 4.4 | 8.3 | 8.4 |
| Wage employment | 8.9 | 11.7 | 12.0 |
|    Private sector | 3.0 | 7.2 | 7.8 |
|    Public sector | 5.9 | 4.5 | 4.2 |
| Total | 100 | 100 | 100 |

*Source:* IAF 1996–97, 2002–03; IOF 2008–09.

activity. Growth in demand for labor from private enterprises has only kept up with the growth of the labor force since 2003 so there was little mobility into this sector.

***Owing to constraints outside the labor market, demand from private employers is not likely to increase rapidly.*** When asked if they would like to increase employment, business owners reported that the main constraints to investment in enterprise growth are not in the labor market, but in the infrastructure sector, in the land and financial markets, and in government rules and regulations, including taxation (World Bank 2009). These constraints could be released through policy and institutional change, as well as through investments in infrastructure, but this process takes time. Even if demand for labor were to double the growth rate of the past—say, twice the rate of growth of the labor force, implying a much higher rate of investment in labor-intensive plants than has been realized in the past—this would result in only about 10 percent of the labor force being employed in such jobs in 15 years. After 25 years of solid, broad-based economic growth and development, Mozambique might expect that nearly 20 percent of the labor force might have this type of employment as their main activity.

This conclusion is based simply on current initial conditions and the high growth rate of the labor force. With the labor force growing at nearly 3 percent per annum, wage and salary employment would need to increase by about 20 percent *yearly* for the next 10 years simply to absorb the majority of new entrants while leaving the existing labor force in their current jobs. This would be about 8 times faster growth than this type of employment achieved in 2002–03 to 2008–09, which is why it is considered highly unlikely.

## Household Enterprises and Poverty Reduction

Thus, for the foreseeable future, Mozambique will be a country of household farms and firms—what is often called "informal economic activity." The transition of labor into non-farm sectors will take place within the scope of household economic activities. Households will be compelled both to raise the productivity of their traditional activity, agriculture, and to add new and more productive "household enterprises" (HEs), or non-farm household businesses (see box 5.1). Thirteen percent of Mozambican households report earning income from HEs in 2008. But this is well behind countries like Ghana, Tanzania, and Uganda, where 40–60 percent of households earn income from this source (Fox and Pimhidzai 2011). In these countries, the HE sector grew because households added a non-farm activity to their agricultural livelihood, spending work time in both agriculture and non-agriculture economic activities.

In low-income Sub-Saharan Africa, it is not known whether labor productivity is higher for households in their non-farm activities, but it is known from studies in other countries that earnings tend to be higher

---

**Box 5.1**

### Household Enterprises

A household enterprise (HE) is a small enterprise not legally separated from other household economic activities. It is usually conducted by a single (own-account) entrepreneur employing only unpaid family members, although outside labor is sometimes employed on a casual basis. Such non-farm HEs are at the lower end of the spectrum of micro, small, and medium enterprises (MSMEs), and are largest in number among MSMEs, but the smallest and most vulnerable. Typical HE activities include selling household goods or clothing in the market, brickmaking and construction, charcoal production, grain milling or other basic agricultural processing, tailoring, hairdressing, making and selling food, running a bar or small restaurant, making furniture, or running a messenger, bicycle, or taxi service.

The HE sector plays an important role in income and job creation in Sub-Saharan Africa. However, the sector is largely ignored in policy and institutional frameworks in most African countries, which generally focus on small and medium enterprises. Mozambique is no exception in this regard.

*Source:* Fox and Pimhidzai 2011.

on average (Fox and Gaal 2008). This trend has been confirmed for Mozambique (Fox et al. 2008; Andre and Fox 2011). These two studies for Mozambique have also confirmed that in discreet periods in the last decade, households that added a household enterprise have higher consumption growth than those that did not, indicating a strong connection with poverty reduction.

> *Education is the key to better economic opportunities and poverty reduction.*

The above employment analysis has important implications for education policy in Mozambique. Many studies of income growth in rural and urban Mozambique have shown the importance of even a few years of education in raising household welfare at the level of the poverty line in both rural and urban areas. For example, Fox et al. (2008) found that a few years of primary education raised household consumption per capita in rural areas by 6 percent and in urban areas by 12 percent in 2003. Completing EP1 basically doubled this effect. Education helped improve household livelihood patterns in various ways: it made the household more efficient in the use of its labor resources and it enabled mobility into new, higher productivity sectors. As noted, diversification of the economic activities of at least one family member out of agriculture was strongly associated with higher household welfare.

## Education Needs of the Labor Force

*How much education does the future labor force need in order to enter the non-farm sector, either through wage employment or by creating a non-farm HE?* As already noted, wage employment opportunities are expected to be quite limited for at least the next 15 years. Mozambique's wage and salary labor force has one of the lowest levels of education in East and Southern Africa. Upgrading of skills in this employment segment would likely enhance competitiveness.

Fortunately, increased enrollment in schools seems to be having an effect on the qualifications of the labor force. Analysis of the IOF surveys showed that over 80 percent of the labor force under 25 who reported working in a wage or salary job (that is, recent hires) had completed at least lower secondary education in 2008. This statistic suggests that in the future secondary education is likely to be the minimum qualification for attainment of a wage and salary job. But it may also suggest that the current supply of secondary schools is providing enough qualified workers given current sluggish demand.

Indeed, it is not obvious that the wage and salary sector is actually absorbing all the secondary graduates who would like to enter the sector, nor that it *could* absorb all the projected future graduates given current trends in labor demand. Surveys of business owners on new hiring suggest that at least for the next few years the education system may be creating more secondary graduates than the wage and salary sector can absorb. This does not mean that these graduates have all the skills that employers seek or that there are no problems with the quality of secondary education. However, these are separate issues. What business owners report is that there are other constraints to the expansion of employment, outside the labor market, that are driving their decisions at present. Further analysis of this question, including analysis of employment data by age and skill level from panels of firms, would be helpful.

Cross-section data from the IOF surveys indicate that some education, at least at a lower level, is needed to operate an HE. For those who declared the HE to be their primary employment, half in 2008 had completed at least EP1, and only 11 percent reported no education at all. But cross-section data do not indicate how important education is relative to other variables correlated in the study, such as the wealth of the household, and they also exclude those for whom an HE is a secondary activity. From the NPS panel data, further insight on the importance of education was gained by looking at the characteristics of the individuals and the households who started a household enterprise between 2002 and 2008.

The analysis confirmed that those who started an enterprise had higher levels of education. Further analysis using NPS data for 2008 of the factors present in 2003 that determined whether a household started an enterprise showed, surprisingly, that wealth was not important. A household could start and sustain a household enterprise from nothing if the adult household members had enough education. Thus, education was the key factor in allowing a household to shift into the non-farm sector with the probability of a higher income and more positive growth path.

These results suggest that the low education level of the labor force is slowing the growth of these HEs, thus reducing the pace of poverty reduction. Adults lacking numeracy cannot start even a rudimentary trading enterprise as they are unable to engage effectively with customers or suppliers, nor can they absorb even the most basic vocational or enterprise training. Although the education progress reported here is gradually raising the qualifications of

Mozambique's workforce, still less than 50 percent of women ages 15–25 (the age of new labor force entrants) in 2009 had even completed EP1 (see figure 5.1). Most of these women will be trapped in the lowest productivity activities, even as they are raising the next generation.

The reforms initiated in 2004–05 are working to alleviate this situation. As these children grow up and transition into the labor force these figures should improve, as will be demonstrated by simulations in the next chapter. But these results show the urgency of effectively addressing the remaining supply-side and demand-side obstacles to greater school enrollment and completion, especially for girls.

In summary, Mozambique's current growth rate in secondary education graduates appears to be ample to meet the demand for educated labor for wage and salary jobs, in part owing to slow growth in demand. This is likely to be the case for the near future, as the number of secondary graduates (especially ES1) is expanding rapidly, even though the starting base is low. In the medium term, if Mozambique is able to release the constraints firms face in expanding, the result should be higher

**Figure 5.1  Education Levels of New Workforce Entrants, 1997, 2003, 2009**

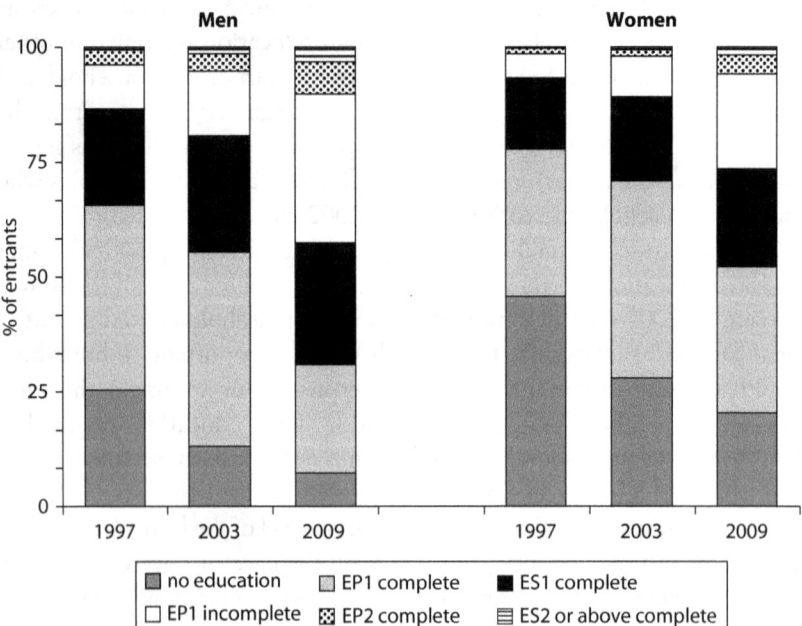

*Sources:* IAF 1996–97, 2002–03; IOF 2008–09.

demand for secondary graduates. But even a major expansion in demand will still not absorb a significant number of new graduates in the labor force in the near future.

The underdeveloped non-farm household enterprise sector is much better placed to provide employment opportunities, and should be able to expand substantially if policies and support are instituted that create a more conducive environment with regard to infrastructure, market locations, and access to finance. This expansion could employ a major share of the labor force and contribute to poverty reduction.

However, expanding HEs would require a major push to increase completion rates for primary education before entering the labor market, especially for girls. The demand-side constraints released by the 2004–05 reforms have supported major progress toward this goal, but Mozambique's poor primary completion record, especially for girls, hinders further progress. As employment in this sector does not appear to be constrained by demand, education for this sector should be an immediate priority.

## Notes

1. This section is based on Andre and Fox (2011).
2. This objective and the official targets are described in the Government of Mozambique's two poverty reduction strategies, called *Plan of Action for the Reduction of Absolute Poverty* (PARPA, in Portuguese) (MPD 2006). PARPA documents and donor comments are available in English at: http://www.imf.org/external/pubs/ft/scr/2011/cr11132.pdf.

## References

Andre, P., and L. Fox. 2011. "Does the Pattern of Education Expansion Matter for Shared Growth and Poverty Reduction? Evidence from Mozambique." Unpublished manuscript. Washington, DC.

Fox, L., R. M. Benfica, M. Ehrenpreis, M. S. Gaal, H. Nordang, and D. Owen. 2008. *Beating the Odds: Sustaining Inclusion in a Growing Economy: A Mozambique Poverty, Gender, and Social Assessment.* Report 40048-MZ. Washington, DC: World Bank.

Fox, L., and M. Gaal. 2008. *Working Out of Poverty: Job Creation and the Quality of Growth in Africa.* Washington, DC: World Bank.

Fox, L., and O. Pimhidzai. 2011. "Is Informality Welfare-Enhancing Structural Transformation? Evidence from Uganda." Policy Research Working Paper 5866, World Bank, Washington, DC.

MPD (Ministério da Planificação e Desenvolvimento). 2006. *Plano de Acçao para a Reducao da Pobreza Absoluta* (PARPAII). Government of Mozambique, Maputo, Mozambique. Available in English at: http://www.imf.org/external/pubs/ft/scr/2011/cr11132.pdf.

———. 2010. *Relatório da 3ª Avaliação da Pobreza Nacional*. Unpublished manuscript, Government of Mozambique, Maputo, Mozambique.

World Bank. 2009. "Investment Climate Assessment, Mozambique." Report 51326, World Bank, Washington, DC.

CHAPTER 6

# Investing in Education: Tough Choices Ahead

Sustaining inclusive economic growth to reach middle-income status is a difficult and long-term endeavor for a country as poor as Mozambique. It is well known that education plays a key role in economic growth (World Bank 2011). By improving worker productivity, supporting more informed livelihood choices, and enabling better management of household activities, education helps adults become better parents and responsible citizens and leads to longer and healthier lives. Education is particularly important for development of low-income countries because it is the key supply-side factor supporting the transformation of household livelihoods and the growth of non-farm employment. In helping move the labor force out of traditional agriculture into higher productivity activities, education supports inclusive growth. In sum, education determines opportunities.

While Mozambique has made great strides in recent years to improve access to primary education, particularly for its most disadvantaged populations, it will need to do more to ensure it has a qualified labor force that can both meet the skill demands in the economy and promote economic growth. This chapter suggests policy options for further reforms that will continue to expand Mozambique's education system, address issues of efficiency and quality, and overcome the pressures on the country's secondary education system.

The findings discussed in this volume suggest that even though primary school enrollment has been rising since at least 1997, the primary level reforms of 2004–05 have been responsible for enrollment increases across the board, but particularly of children ages 8–10, those in rural areas, and girls. However, despite improvements in enrollment, overall efficiency in the education system remains low. Most children who enter lower primary do not complete this education level at the appropriate age. Even fewer of them advance to upper primary and beyond. And many children who should be in school are not. Higher fees and longer distances to schools impede access to EP2 for poor and vulnerable children, especially in rural areas.

The expansion of primary education resulting from the reforms made for a more inclusive system, but because of limited resources, it also put enormous pressure on quality. Pupil-teacher ratios have soared in some areas, and achievement results indicate a potential deterioration in student learning. Although according to the various surveys, parents seem happy with the reforms overall, especially cost reduction, many remain skeptical about other aspects such as semi-automatic passing. Most parents also complain about poor learning environments in schools.

The greater enrollment and retention at the lower levels created by the primary reforms have increased secondary school enrollment. However, the network of public secondary schools, though much larger today, is still limited, and the cost of secondary schooling remains a key deterrent. It is at this level that private schools play a very important role in providing education.

## Policy Tradeoffs and the General Question of Access

The question of access to education is a crucial one for Mozambique. If the country seeks to promote inclusive growth and be more competitive in the region, it will have to catch up to its neighbors and increase the number of primary graduates and overall educational attainment. It is imperative that all new labor force entrants have at least a complete lower primary education (that is, passing 5 grades) and that as many as possible have a complete primary education in order to make the transition from low productivity traditional agriculture to higher productivity non-farm sectors. This means that the country must adopt additional measures on the demand side to reach those still not in the system and address the apparent demand-side barriers in upper primary. At the same time, as more students complete primary school, they are likely to demand spaces in affordable secondary schools, either publicly or privately provided. The rest of this study addresses what will be needed to meet these competing pressures.

Improving the education level of the labor force is a long process. Despite the tremendous progress made in the last decade, still in 2008 a third of the labor force had not gone to school at all, primarily because most current workers entered the labor force without qualifications when access to education was very limited. The share of workers in the labor force with no formal education will continue declining as the older generation ages out of the workforce and the generations benefitting from the increased educational opportunities achieved to date enter the labor force. But big changes in the share without education will only be seen in the next decade owing to the high number of people age 30 and above without education.

Some progress in improving the qualifications of the labor force is apparent as the early post-war achievements in education access begin to show up in the labor force. Between 2003 and 2008, the share of the labor force over 20 years of age with complete lower primary education or higher increased from 28 to 31 percent, and the share with completed full primary education rose from 12 to 19 percent.

Is Mozambique on track to supply a labor force with the minimum qualifications to make the transition to higher productivity farm and non-farm activities? To analyze this question, a simulation was run of what the qualifications of the labor force would look like if the current rate of transition through the education system continues. The simulation model is described in appendix B and the results are shown in figures 6.1 and 6.2. These figures show the projected distribution of the labor force among workers ranging from those with less than complete EP1 to those with higher level qualifications.

Assuming the current rate of efficiency and transition, Mozambique can likely expect a fairly large increase in the share of the labor force completing primary education: an increase of 1 percent per year between 2008 and 2013 (see table A.22). And the share of workers with higher qualifications increases quite rapidly and stays high because there are very few older workers in this group. The share of the labor force ages 25–29 with complete ES1 or above increased from 2.4 percent in 2003 to 12.3 percent in 2008 and is projected to be 21 percent in 2013. Overall, if current trends continue, of those with education in the labor

**Figure 6.1 Observed and Projected Distribution of Labor Force by Education Level, 2008 and 2013**

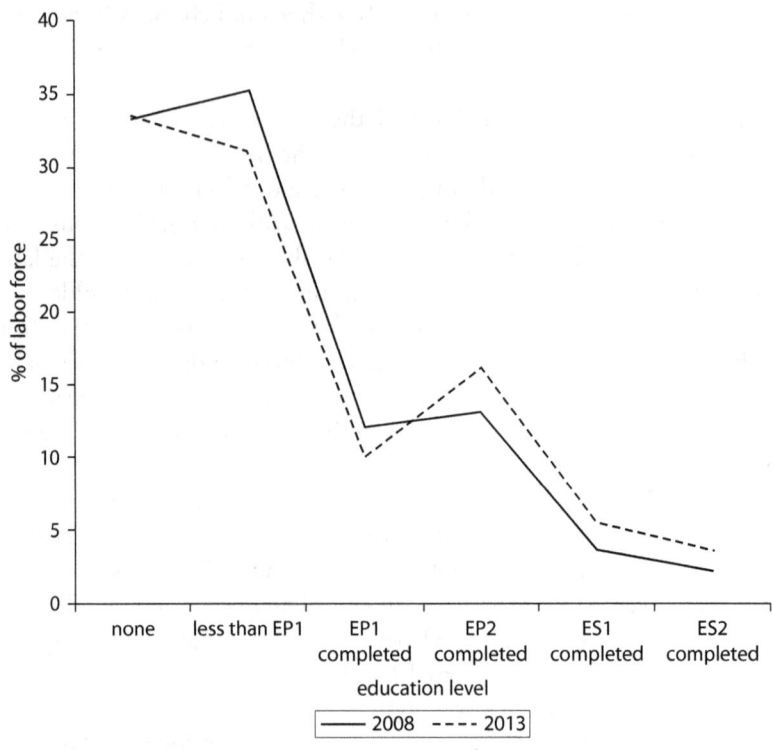

*Sources:* NPS 2008 and IAF 2003; see table A.2.

force, 25 percent would have completed primary (EP2) or above by 2013 and 9 percent would have completed lower secondary (ES1) or above.

Can Mozambique do better than this projection if suitable policies were to be put in place? The country could move these numbers along faster by increasing transitions to higher grade levels. To achieve this the country might build even more schools and train even more teachers, as well as develop programs and policies to improve system efficiency by reducing repetitions and increasing completions. Or a combination of the two policies could be put in place.

Figure 6.2 (and table A.22) show projections of the changes in the labor force that might result from increasing transitions first within primary levels only, and then within secondary levels only. If the policy choices resulted in a doubling of primary transition rates, by 2013 the share of the labor force completing EP2 (or above) would rise from 25 to

**Figure 6.2 Projected Distribution of Labor Force with Increased Transition Rates at Primary and Secondary Levels, 2013**

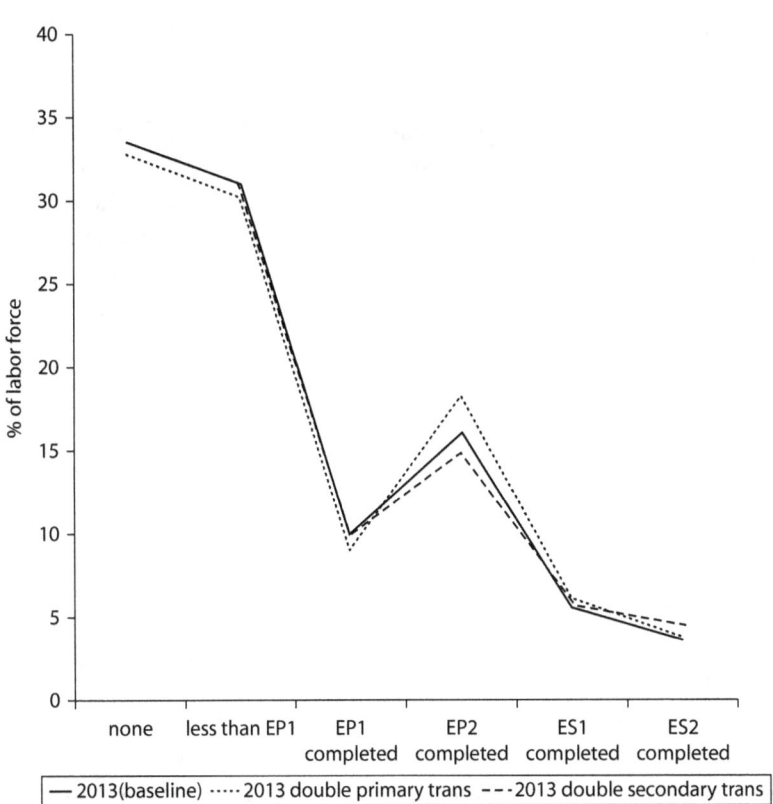

*Sources:* NPS 2008 and IAF 2003; see table A.2.

28 percent—an impressive increase over the already projected increase of 6 percentage points given current transition rates. Given that completion of this level seems critical for livelihood diversification, making the effort to improve primary transitions seems worthwhile. There would be a spillover to the secondary transition rates anyway (assuming minor capacity expansion under current growth policies plus some efficiency improvements); the percentage of the educated labor force with completed lower secondary (ES1) would then rise from 9.1 to 9.7. On the other hand, if the policy choices left the rate of transition in primary the same but focused on expanding secondary enrollments, there would be only a modest increase in the share of the labor force that completes at least lower secondary compared to the "double primary" transition, from 9.7 percent to

10.3. The transition from lower to upper secondary shows a bigger jump than in the "double primary rates" scenario, of course.

## Emphasize Primary or Secondary?

All of these scenarios suggest that increasing the qualifications of the labor force requires a long-term strategy. But the scenarios also shed light on one of Mozambique's key strategic choices, that is, whether to focus on increasing completion of primary school or secondary school.

Mozambique will have to make tradeoffs in strategies to solve the problem today. Increasing transition rates and completions in primary schooling is relatively cheap, as the system does not seem to be highly supply constrained. This is especially true for the transition from EP1 to EP2. While it is obviously important for investments in facilities and inputs to keep up with the growth of the school-age population, the results projected above could be achieved at a low cost, through increasing efficiency in the use of existing facilities so that more students complete primary school. Modest demand-side measures to decrease dropout should help as well.

Above EP2 in secondary education, the system is highly capacity constrained, so rapid achievement of the highest transition ratios projected probably would require expansion in supply as well as efficiency improvements and demand side measures to move even more children through the system. This would be much more costly. So improving access and efficiency at the primary level might have nearly the same effect on the number of secondary grads simply through increasing the pool of students eligible for secondary education, and it would be a more equitable way to achieve the same goal.

Of course, this result assumes that the additional primary graduates would have the same propensity to attend secondary as those in the past. This might not be the case, however, as the incremental primary school graduates might come from lower income or more remote households that are short on the resources required. But policy could address this through targeted subsidies, which would be cheaper than a broad program of public secondary education expansion.

In working through these options, it is important to keep in mind not only the issue of quantity but also quality. The tradeoff is not only between investment in facilities on one level over another. It also involves investments in quality of classroom experience at all levels. But again, boosting quality in primary levels could improve retention and thus increase the number transitioning from lower into upper primary, and on to secondary (see box 6.1).

It is also important to keep in mind the role of the public sector in providing access to education for those who might not be able to get it any other way. Chapter 3 indicated that demand for secondary schooling in Mozambique is at least partially being met through private education. Public policy could support this trend, for example, by providing scholarships for the private system rather than building more public schools.

Questions for policy makers to consider are as follows:

1. Who needs to attend low-cost schooling at an appropriate distance or they will not attend at all? When does the public sector need to supply these schools because the private sector will not (for example, remote areas, students with special needs, and so forth)?
2. At which level are the private returns of education high enough that individuals or families can finance their own education?
3. How can the country make use of targeted schemes, such as scholarships or loans to alleviate credit constraints that might prevent some individuals from obtaining further schooling or from accessing higher quality services abroad (for example for higher education)?

Policy makers should also consider the relative costs of providing education at each level. Per student costs in secondary schools are more than double those in primary schools.[1] Considering the scope of the public sector and alternative means of providing education where it becomes more costly and less inclusive might make it easier for policy makers to compare the costs and potential benefits of various policy options.

## Policy Options for Mozambique

The analysis in this volume highlights six issues to be addressed as Mozambique moves into the next stage of education policy: (1) how to get children into primary school on time; (2) how to raise the transition rates; (3) how to raise quality; (4) how to measure and track system performance in real time; (5) where to expand the system using public funds; and (6) how to ensure that youth who leave school are ready for work.

Recommendations for how Mozambique can begin addressing these issues are as follows.

> **Box 6.1**
>
> ## Two Common Tradeoffs in Education Policy
>
> When resources are constrained, it helps to highlight two major tradeoffs that policy makers usually face when considering investments in education.
>
> **Quality vs. Quantity.** Even though economies of scale in education mean that one teacher can probably just as easily teach 15 children as 5, when education systems expand, significant resources are needed to ensure that quality does not fall. This is particularly the case if the expansion reaches previously underserved populations for two reasons. First, most children of school age that are out of school are from poorer families with little or no education background. Often these children have had difficulty in school and dropped out early. Educating these children, therefore, will be more costly. Second, most education systems begin by expanding supply where it is less costly and economies of scale are greater, such as urban areas. Expanding access to rural and remote regions is more costly both because building and operating schools can be expensive and because the number of children at an appropriate distance from school is smaller. Investments in supply could come at the cost of quality if resources are not increased or used more efficiently, or if quality management systems are not in place. Countries must
>
> *(continued next page)*

### *On-Time Entrance*

1. **The fastest way to ensure higher coverage of primary education is to ensure that children start school on time.**

Even though evidence suggests that the 2004–05 reforms motivated younger children to enroll in school, the problem of late entry remains. Studies show that children achieve more if they start primary school at the official school-entry age of 6 years, because they are more likely to complete primary school, they learn more at a young age, and having older and younger children in the same classroom can be disruptive (see Wils 2004). Despite the benefits of enrolling in school early, a large proportion of 6- and 7-year-old children, over 60 percent and 40 percent respectively, are out of school. And, when asked why their 6- and 7-year-old children are not in school, most parents answered that they were "not of school age" (see figure 3.11).

**Box 6.1** *(continued)*

decide what standard of quality is acceptable as they continue to expand access. It is also important to ensure that this same standard of quality is available to all schools in the country, and not just those in urban or other better-off areas.

**Primary vs. Secondary.** Investment in primary education, especially in a young country such as Mozambique, will be more progressive, that is, will reach more children, particularly those from low-income households, than investment in secondary education. The reason is simple: even if the schooling is free, most low-income students cannot afford the opportunity cost of remaining in school once they are of working age. In addition, primary schools tend to require fewer resources than secondary schools because learning at this level is less specialized. On the other hand, as countries begin to grow economically, the demand for higher level skills and knowledge will grow. Moreover, it is difficult to sustain quality higher education and teacher training without a sufficient number of qualified secondary school graduates. Finally, the parents of children who access secondary education and beyond will tend to have more "voice." Countries facing pressures to expand supply and remove demand-side barriers must keep in mind the populations most likely to be served and benefitted at each education level.

*Source:* Authors.

Mozambique should closely study the reasons for late entry. Reasons could range from nutrition issues to lack of knowledge and awareness of the benefits of starting early to concerns about the safety of young children walking on the roads and pathways to school. Policies should respond to the reasons for this behavior and could include options such as community awareness programs on the importance of starting school on time or even making school entrance mandatory at age 6.

In a number of countries, including Mozambique, Early Childhood Development programs have been shown to support on-time entrance to primary education and result in better learning outcomes (see box 6.2). In other countries, conditional cash transfer programs (CCT) have been used (see box 6.3). For lower primary, where financial reasons are not the main reason children do not start school on time, CCTs would still provide a financial incentive to send children to school. Mozambique is now developing strategies in both areas. But both of these options involve major new expenditures at a time of limited resources, so cost-effectiveness

> **Box 6.2**
>
> **Would Early Childhood Development (ECD) Programs in Mozambique Get Children to Start School on Time?**
>
> It is well-known that the years up to age 5 are most important for learning, as many of the foundational cognitive and motor skills needed for learning are formed during this period. Failure to develop these foundational skills during the window of opportunity of early childhood can lead to long-term, often irreversible effects. Hence, the traditional view of education starting with primary school takes up the challenge too late. During the early years of life, children need a supportive learning environment including health care, proper nutrition, and a stimulating environment to support cognitive development (World Bank 2011).
>
> A 2008 study conducted by the Mozambique Government, Save the Children, and the World Bank on a sample of children ages 3–5 in 72 poor rural communities in Gaza province, found that, too often, these key learning prerequisites are not being built during children's first five years (World Bank 2010). The study found that 42 percent of surveyed children were stunted and the majority of the children demonstrated significant cognitive development delays. The study also found low school preparedness among children in the sample. These developmental delays might partly explain why poor children are less likely to start school on time in Mozambique.
>
> Pilot programs organized by donors and nongovernmental organizations have shown that low-cost, community-based ECD intervention can yield positive results in the specific context of rural Mozambique. While current results are still preliminary, they indicate that children ages 3–5 who participated in a
>
> *(continued next page)*

is a critical issue. Further data collection from parents on the reasons for late entry and careful analysis of actual outcomes from pilot program experiences should guide further efforts.

### *Raising Transition Rates*
2. **Primary students must also transition effectively and efficiently through the system and complete their studies.**

Improving access to primary school is important, but so is making sure that children stay in school and complete each level satisfactorily. To support improvements in labor force productivity, income growth, and

**Box 6.2** *(continued)*

community ECD intervention in rural Gaza performed better on measures of cognitive and overall development at age 6 than those in the control group and that they are more likely to enter primary school at the right age than the control group.

The Ministry of Education (MOE) has recognized the importance of ECD for Mozambique. In March 2011, the MOE established an ECD Secretariat in the Directorate for Primary Education and appointed an ECD commission tasked with the responsibility of drafting a multi-sectoral ECD strategy for Mozambique. One issue is that most of the pilots developed to date are "full service," including a center, trained and paid teachers, nutritious meal services, and so on. However, funding for scale-up of this type of pilot project in Mozambique is unavailable. Even more important, local administration and monitoring is inadequate to undertake the additional responsibility of ECD without adequate preparation.

Supported by donors, the new ECD strategy plans to focus on *community-supported* pre-school models that could be established in poor areas with initially limited inputs from the Ministry of Education and Culture (for example, staff training, provision of learning materials, and in poor areas, financing of some recurrent costs). It should be noted that cost per child in ECD is normally less than one-half that of primary school. So if ECD by improving readiness, reduces dropouts and repetition in EP1, it will be a good investment. However, it will be critical for planners of the strategy to develop further pilots that focus on one intervention at a time, to identify the most important program elements needed to get children into primary school and learning.

*Source:* World Bank 2010.

poverty reduction, Mozambique should meet the challenge of raising primary school completion as soon as possible.

It is likely that both demand-side and supply-side barriers affect smooth grade-to-grade progression and completion. Reducing the demand-side barriers to starting children in school at the appropriate age should help. But still many parents complain of lack of spaces in lower and upper primary schools, and even without official school fees, many families find it difficult to send their children to upper primary because of the distance to the nearest school (and the costs this implies). Repetition rates are high, particularly in 5th grade and in upper primary and these also might be related to dropouts at these levels.

> **Box 6.3**
>
> ## Conditional Cash Transfers in Mozambique: A Simulation Exercise
>
> Recently praised as successful in alleviating current and long-term poverty, conditional cash transfers (CCT)—regular cash payments to poor families on the condition that their children attend school—may be a beneficial alternative to boost school enrollment in Mozambique. The success of the CCT depends on the program being well targeted and having adequate size of payments, as well as on the schools being able to absorb new enrollment. The following exercise simulates the impact of a CCT program to stimulate enrollment for poor Mozambican children ages 6–14 years by reducing income constraints.[1]
>
> For the purposes of this simulation, the CCT benefit amount is either Mt 100 (US$4) or Mt 200 (US$7.50) a month in 2008 local currency units, (about 8 or 15 percent of the consumption of the bottom quintile). The poorest 10, 20, or 30 percent of the rural population (according to the consumption distribution) have been selected as beneficiaries.[2] Transfers are fixed per household and a pro-rata penalty (household transfer divided by number of eligible children) is applied for each child who does not attend school. The simulation analysis provides a measure of whether households can respond positively to a CCT designed to mitigate impacts of current poverty in the short run and increase human capital in the long run.
>
> *(continued next page)*

While the supply of schools in both lower and upper primary expanded considerably in the past decade, access to upper primary and higher levels remains a problem. These supply constraints might be one of the reasons why fees and other costs remain high in upper primary. The Government should make sure to continue to expand and upgrade the network of lower primary schools in rural areas and upper primary schools in both rural and urban areas.

To ease demand-side barriers, further lowering of costs and fees in upper primary should be considered. CCTs could also be considered as a way of reducing the indirect cost of schooling for lower income families (box 6.3). The opportunity cost of schooling becomes relevant in upper primary. CCTs could ensure this opportunity cost is significantly lowered, allowing children to remain in and finish school.

**Box 6.3** *(continued)*

**Impact of the CCT on School Enrollment, Children Ages 6–14, in Rural Areas, 2008**

| | Target Population | | | | | |
|---|---|---|---|---|---|---|
| | Poorest 10% | | Poorest 20% | | Poorest 30% | |
| Benefit amount | Actual enrollment % | Estimated enrollment % | Actual enrollment % | Estimated enrollment % | Actual enrollment % | Estimated enrollment % |
| Mt 100 | 63.5 | 68.3 ($\Delta$=7.6) | 64.0 | 68.2 ($\Delta$=6.6) | 65.6 | 70.3 ($\Delta$=7.1) |
| Mt 200 | 63.5 | 73.1 ($\Delta$=15.1) | 64.0 | 71.5 ($\Delta$=11.7) | 65.6 | 72.4 ($\Delta$=10.4) |

*Source:* Authors' calculation from NPS 2008 data.

Conclusions that can be drawn from the simulation are: (1) CCTs would have a positive impact on school enrollment for all poor children in rural areas; (2) CCT program impact would be larger for poor children ages 6–9, motivating them to enroll early in EP1; (3) higher benefits would lead to larger impacts, but at the cost of increasing program cost; (4) CCT program cost would be lower than 0.5% of GDP, depending on the combination of benefit amount and beneficiary population; and (5) to increase demand for schooling among the poor, funds should be paid directly to the household.

*Source:* Leite 2011.
1. Simulation uses an ex-ante model such as the one detailed in Bourguignon, Ferreira, and Leite (2003).
2. Actual implementation of a CCT program would select beneficiaries on the basis of declared income, proxy-means test, community targeting, or a combination of methods.

As long as significant supply constraints exist, however, demand-side policies such as CCTs or others will not have the intended effects. Mozambique should consider exploring further the reasons for noncompletion, as well as the reasons for high repetition rates in 5$^{th}$ grade as well as in the upper primary level.

### Raising Education Quality Level
3. **Quality needs to be closely monitored, particularly as the system continues to grow and become more inclusive.**

Primary school is an important tool for an individual's economic progress in the country. Despite the positive improvements to expand access, achievements in primary education remain below the requirements for Mozambique's economy. Put simply, the quality of the education must be improved so students learn more during their time in school.

The poor quality of many lower primary schools might also be driving people away. There is a dire need to improve school infrastructure, particularly in rural areas. While class size itself may not be the major source of low quality, it is unlikely that the reported class size of more than 70 students in some areas could be conducive to learning. Finally, all students should have access to books and other materials at free or reduced cost so they can take the most advantage of their time in school.

Curriculum reforms should be evaluated to make sure that teachers are sufficiently trained to deal with the new curriculum. Semi-automatic passing should not be seen as an opportunity to cruise along for a number of years but as a way to ensure that students are given sufficient time to understand the subject matter without being unnecessarily held back.

Expanding access without compromising quality to the point of reducing the value of a primary school education should be the objective going forward.

### *Tracking System Performance*
4. **Measuring and monitoring performance at national and local levels can unlock performance problems.**

Meeting quality and quantity challenges requires continuous monitoring of education expenditures and results, including inputs such as quality of school infrastructure, teacher performance, and availability of books and other learning tools as well as student outputs (learning hours) and outcomes. Monitoring of local program implementation, such as the imposition of fees, is important to ensure that they do not continue to pose a barrier to entry and completion.

In a large and predominantly rural country like Mozambique, effective monitoring must be done close to the point of service delivery, at the school level. The distance of the central government from the point of delivery means that local governments in Mozambique need to increasingly take an active role in monitoring. Parents and the wider local communities can also provide effective feedback to governments. Information coming from the ground needs to be systematic, easy to collect, and comparable across jurisdictions.

The current system of top-down monitoring is expensive and not effective enough. This study found a large variation in fees paid by households, which may or may not be related to the quality of education received by the students. Meanwhile, parents report that community school committees are not used for regular feedback to the local or central government. Administrative data are routinely collected but not accurately reported and do not provide adequate information to improve education services.

A more efficient approach is to develop a simple national monitoring system to be implemented at the local government level, with inputs from parents, teachers, students, and school committees. Such a system would allow benchmarking at the facility, district, and province levels, and would set up an accountability mechanism that can build trust between the schools and the community as well as hold principals and district officials increasingly accountable for outcomes. Mozambique will need to explore this type of local, demand-driven monitoring as a complement to policy reforms.

### *Funding Decisions on System Expansion*
5. **Options to expand secondary schooling should be determined relative to the issues remaining in primary.**

As primary enrollment continues to rise and if efficiency improves, the country will face serious supply challenges, particularly in the upper levels and in rural areas, increasing the pressure to expand secondary schooling. In considering these challenges, the Mozambique Government should also note that operating costs per student in secondary school are two to three times higher than in primary school, investment costs are up to 16 times higher, and teacher training is more expensive as well. Mozambique will face tough choices as it strives to improve access to education for its population, particularly those at greater disadvantage, while at the same time improving the possibility of any individual student progressing to the next education level. Solutions other than public school construction can be examined. The Government should examine the experience of countries such as Bangladesh, where most of its secondary education is privately provided.

For its future strategy, the Government should do a cost analysis of how to ensure more secondary school graduates, looking at budget tradeoffs on the supply side; the role of increasing access, efficiency, and quality in primary school in achieving this goal; and the implications for equity, employment opportunities, wealth creation, and poverty reduction of the various options.

## *Ensuring Readiness for Work*
6. Making sure youth who leave school are ready for work.

For the next 10 years, most Mozambican youth who enter the economy seeking productive employment will need to make their own livelihoods, either working on their family farm or creating a business that sells goods or services to their community or to another small business. The Government should strive to make sure that these youth are ready for work. This starts with making sure that as many children as possible finish school with competency in the basic subjects, but it also involves teaching behaviors and competencies that will allow them to find productive economic activities and make these activities pay. It is most efficient to do this while they are in school, before they have dispersed into their communities and beyond.

The primary school curriculum is currently oriented to teaching basic skills and preparing kids for secondary school. However, owing both to supply constraints and the high cost of education at this level, most Mozambican children cannot progress onto secondary school. For many of them, primary education will be all that they get. Yet, they graduate from upper primary unprepared to generate their own employment opportunities—indeed, even possibly unaware of such opportunities and how to take advantage of them. Evidence from other countries suggests that post-school training is expensive, unlikely to reach this group of people, and has a low payoff.

All of this suggests a need to make primary school as valuable and productive for children as it can be. This can be done, for example, by supplementing the basic skills curriculum with financial literacy and other practical, competency-based subjects that can serve youngsters well in the workplace. These modules do not need to be extensive; evidence suggests that teaching basic "rules of thumb" can make a difference given minimal numeracy skills (see box 6.4). Testing and evaluating new curriculum options in this area should be a high priority.

## Education in Mozambique: A Bright Future

Mozambique has come a long way in improving access to lower and upper primary schools through sustained investment in education infrastructure and introduction of important reforms. To its credit, Mozambique was able to conduct a massive school infrastructure program while implementing bold reforms to improve access to primary education for millions

> **Box 6.4**
>
> ## "Rules of Thumb" Financial Training Can Improve Business Management for Household and Micro Entrepreneurs
>
> Teaching financial literacy to small-scale entrepreneurs as a strategy to improve their money management, business strategies, earnings, and profits has received increased attention in developing countries. Several studies have documented a strong association between household well-being and the understanding of financial concepts through better financial decision making. But how can training programs effectively reach the huge numbers of household and micro enterprises in low income Africa who are primary school leavers? Can simple but effective courses be designed and rolled out for all who need them?
>
> A recent study on teaching financial concepts finds convincing evidence that teaching simple rules of thumb is an affordable method that leads to good results. The study, which took place in the Dominican Republic, conducted a randomized control trial on the efficacy of two types of financial training programs: (1) the standard approach—a classroom course using traditional principles-based financial training in basic accounting techniques and (2) a short rule of thumb course that covered simple rules for financial decisions such as keeping separate business and personal accounts. The latter is suitable for participants without secondary education, for example, and is cheaper to teach. The study showed that receiving rule of thumb training produced better results than the more complex and time-consuming principles-based training.
>
> For countries like Mozambique, the study shows that improving financial literacy and decision making of small business owners, such as household enterprise owners (or farmers), is possible and affordable. Programs could be rolled out through night classes for adults. Even more effective would be to add this material to the primary school curriculum. Reaching these future entrepreneurs with this simple and practical material while they are still in school would better prepare primary school graduates to take advantage of economic opportunities as they arise and manage their future incomes and assets.
>
> *Source:* Drexler, Fisher, and Schoar 2010.

of children in the country. Parents responded to the 2004–05 reforms by sending more children to school for a longer time, as they recognized that they needed to respond favorably to the public sector doing its part to improve access. While there is no doubt that further progress is needed, a commitment at both the household level and the government level has been demonstrated to meet these challenges. New targets for the future, such as reaching the education Millennium Development Goal and improving student achievement, have been set in Mozambique's key policy documents, including the new Five-Year Plan and Poverty Reduction Program.

Mozambique has undertaken expansion of access to education as a key policy goal not just as an end in itself, but because the lack of a qualified labor force is a constraint to economic growth and poverty reduction. There is no disagreement that to achieve inclusive growth, the education system must ensure that as many children as possible start and finish primary school with competency in the basic subjects, as well as the skills to allow them to find productive economic activities. At the same time, Mozambique needs to prepare for a needed expansion of secondary education, and for enhanced support to learning and skill development in the early years.

As the country forges ahead, the challenges, and some of the choices, are clear. In some areas, once the strategies and targets are determined, implementation would benefit from more analysis of some of the specific issues. The findings of the present study suggest that the following areas remain to be examined:

- the reasons for late entry, and the cost-effectiveness of possible remedies on the demand side;
- the factors affecting dropout and repetition rates, particularly in the key transitions between lower and upper primary, and upper primary and secondary;
- the skills needed by primary school leavers in order to effectively transition from school to work, and whether these are being adequately taught and developed in primary schools; and
- methods to effectively monitor system performance and improve overall quality in the system.

Further analysis in these areas could help Mozambique make tough choices regarding policy options for the future and implement strategies more effectively.

### Note

1. Per student costs are estimated at around 1,780 Mt for primary and 3,700 Mt for secondary, using 2009 budget figures from MEC, which include salary expenditures.

## References

Bourguignon, F., F.H.G. Ferreira, and P.G. Leite. 2003. "Conditional Cash Transfer, Schooling, and Child Labour: Micro-Simulating Brazil's Bolsa-Escola Program." *The World Bank Economic Review* 17 (2): 229–54.

Drexler, Alejandro, Greg Fisher, and Antoinette S. Schoar. 2010. "Keeping It Simple: Financial Literacy and Rules of Thumb." CEPR Discussion Paper 7994. Centre for Economic Policy Research, London, UK.

Leite, P. 2011. "Increasing Access to Education in Mozambique: The Potential Role of a Conditional Cash Transfer." Unpublished manuscript, World Bank, Washington, DC.

Wils, A. 2004. "Late Entrants Leave School Early: Evidence from Mozambique." *International Review of Education* 50 (1): 17–37.

World Bank. 2010. "Building Evidence on the Impact of Community-Based Pre-Schools in Mozambique. A Collaborative Effort Among Save the Children, the Government of Mozambique, and the World Bank." Unpublished manuscript, World Bank, Washington, DC.

———. 2011. "Learning for All: Investing in People's Knowledge and Skills to Promote Development." World Bank Group Education Strategy 2020. Unpublished manuscript, World Bank, Washington, DC.

**APPENDIXES**

APPENDIX A

# Additional Tables from the Analysis

## Primary Education: Enrollment Rates and Factors Affecting Enrollment

**Table A.1 Gross Enrollment Rates in Primary by Residence Area and Gender, 1997, 2003, and 2008 (% of population)**

|  | Urban | | Rural | | | |
|---|---|---|---|---|---|---|
|  | Male | Female | Male | Female | Total | Growth (%) |
| EP1 | | | | | | |
| 1997 | 89.8 | 83.0 | 75.6 | 50.6 | 67.7 | — |
| 2003 | 113.1 | 109.7 | 104.8 | 86.3 | 100.2 | 48 |
| 2008 | 108.5 | 104.0 | 107.3 | 98.9 | 104.0 | 4 |
| EP2 | | | | | | |
| 1997 | 92.3 | 71.0 | 26.1 | 13.6 | 34.3 | — |
| 2003 | 120.6 | 110.1 | 37.2 | 19.5 | 57.0 | 66 |
| 2008 | 120.2 | 112.2 | 68.6 | 50.0 | 78.5 | 38 |

*Sources:* MICS 2008; IAF 2002–03; IAF 1996–97.
*Note:* The age groups used in this table are the ones used prior to the 2006 change: 6–11 for EP1 and 12–13 for EP2.

**Table A.2 Net Enrollment Rates in Primary by Residence Area and Gender, 1997, 2003, and 2008 (% of population)**

|  | Rural | Urban | Male | Female | Total |
|---|---|---|---|---|---|
| EP1 |  |  |  |  |  |
| 1997 | 34.9 | 56.8 | 42.3 | 36.4 | 39.3 |
| 2003 | 57.7 | 75.9 | 65.1 | 61.2 | 63.1 |
| 2008 | 69.0 | 80.8 | 73.3 | 71.8 | 72.5 |
| EP2 |  |  |  |  |  |
| 1997 | 2.6 | 18.9 | 5.9 | 6.9 | 6.4 |
| 2003 | 4.0 | 19.9 | 9.6 | 8.6 | 9.1 |
| 2008 | 14.0 | 39.7 | 21.4 | 23.9 | 22.6 |

*Sources:* MICS 2008; IAF 2002–03; IAF 1996–97.
*Note:* The age groups used in this table are the ones used prior to the 2006 change: 6–11 for EP1 and 12–13 for EP2.

**Table A.3 Children's Educational Attainment by Age in Primary, 2003 and 2008**

|  | 2003 | | | 2008 | | |
|---|---|---|---|---|---|---|
| Age | Not attending (%) | EP1 (%) | EP2 (%) | Not attending (%) | EP1 (%) | EP2 (%) |
| 6 | 61 | 38.9 | 0.0 | 53.3 | 46.6 | 0.1 |
| 7 | 47 | 52.7 | 0.0 | 29.1 | 70.9 | 0.0 |
| 8 | 34 | 65.2 | 0.3 | 22.8 | 77.1 | 0.1 |
| 9 | 24 | 75.6 | 0.1 | 16.4 | 83.0 | 0.6 |
| 10 | 25 | 73.4 | 1.2 | 16.9 | 81.7 | 1.4 |
| 11 | 18 | 77.8 | 4.4 | 10.6 | 79.1 | 10.3 |
| 12 | 23 | 70.1 | 6.6 | 15.1 | 65.0 | 19.9 |
| 13 | 23 | 63.6 | 12.5 | 18.6 | 55.1 | 26.3 |
| 14 | 29 | 46.8 | 20.2 | 29.2 | 39.2 | 31.6 |
| 15 | 36 | 36.7 | 21.5 | 46.4 | 24.6 | 29.0 |
| 16 | 49 | 22.3 | 19.0 | 57.2 | 15.5 | 27.3 |
| 17 | 53 | 19.2 | 15.5 | 77.1 | 6.3 | 16.6 |
| 18 | 68 | 8.4 | 10.3 | 83.2 | 7.2 | 9.6 |
| 19 | 74 | 4.8 | 7.3 | 93.3 | 1.1 | 5.6 |

*Sources:* MICS 2008; IAF 2002–03; Poverty and Social Impact Analysis (PSIA) 2005.

### Table A.4  Average Transition Rates (% students)

|  | 1999–2003 | 2004–2008 | Total |
|---|---|---|---|
| Last grade EP1 (5th) | 83 | 85 | 84 |
| First grade EP2 (6th) | 70 | 77 | 74 |
| Last grade EP2 (7th) | 74 | 80 | 77 |
| First grade ES1 (8th) | 57 | 63 | 60 |
| Last grade ES1 (10th) | 75 | 74 | 75 |
| First grade ES2 (11th) | 48 | 61 | 54 |

*Source:* NPS 2008, Education History Module.
*Note:* These rates represent average survival rates in the time period for all cohorts. These are average grade-to-grade cohort transition rates. They represent the average of the transition rates observed in table 3.3 for the years observed. They are not "survival" rates. This means that they only average how many of one year's enrollment goes on to the next.

### Table A.5  Reasons for Never Attending or Dropping Out of School (% of respondents mentioning reason), ages 6–19 Years

| Year | Supply-side problems[a] | High cost[b] | Work[c] | Marriage/ pregnancy/ health issues | Not of school age[d] | Others | Total |
|---|---|---|---|---|---|---|---|
| % of respondents | | | | | | | |
| 1998 | 13.3 | 10.3 | 11.6 | 5.1 | 26.2 | 33.4 | 100 |
| 1999 | 13.6 | 11.5 | 10.1 | 4.7 | 29.5 | 30.6 | 100 |
| 2000 | 9.7 | 10.1 | 10.7 | 7.0 | 32.6 | 29.9 | 100 |
| 2001 | 11.7 | 9.6 | 11.8 | 7.2 | 30.8 | 28.9 | 100 |
| 2002 | 11.7 | 9.8 | 11.4 | 7.5 | 30.1 | 29.4 | 100 |
| 2003 | 13.7 | 8.5 | 12.9 | 7.8 | 27.7 | 29.3 | 100 |
| 2004 | 14.5 | 5.1 | 13.5 | 9.1 | 28.7 | 29.1 | 100 |
| 2005 | 12.9 | 5.1 | 12.5 | 10.7 | 25.1 | 33.7 | 100 |
| 2006 | 10.8 | 6.4 | 11.7 | 10.9 | 27.8 | 32.4 | 100 |
| 2007 | 11.6 | 5.7 | 12.2 | 12.2 | 21.0 | 37.2 | 100 |
| 2008 | 13.1 | 4.8 | 13.1 | 10.8 | 16.9 | 41.4 | 100 |
| Total | 12.4 | 7.8 | 12.0 | 8.5 | 27.0 | 32.2 | 100 |
| Avg sample size | 1,483 | 1,160 | 1,460 | 990 | 3,272 | 3,341 | 11,706 |

*Source:* NPS 2008, Education History Module.
a. Supply-side problems include no school vacancy, school is too far away, no good school for the level/grade, the school is closed, no teachers, teacher is not dedicated, and lack of books.
b. High cost includes school fee, uniform costs, and material costs.
c. Work includes work outside the home, on the farm, for the household, take care of sick members, and take care of family.
d. Age corresponds to age in the year of not being enrolled. Population excludes those who last attended school before 1998.

**Table A.6  Reasons for Not Being Enrolled in School, by Age (% respondents mentioning reason), 1998–2008**

| Age of the enrolled year | Supply-side problems[a] | High cost[b] | Work[c] | Marriage/ pregnancy/ health issues | Not of school age[d] | Others | Total |
|---|---|---|---|---|---|---|---|
| 6 | 7.7 | 4.6 | 2.4 | 0.9 | 75.6 | 8.8 | 100 |
| 7 | 11.8 | 8.9 | 6.2 | 1.7 | 57.3 | 14.1 | 100 |
| 8 | 15.6 | 14.2 | 9.2 | 2.5 | 40.4 | 18.1 | 100 |
| 9 | 16.6 | 15.0 | 11.5 | 3.2 | 31.5 | 22.2 | 100 |
| 10 | 17.3 | 15.1 | 12.4 | 3.8 | 24.7 | 26.7 | 100 |
| 11 | 17.4 | 13.5 | 14.1 | 5.3 | 21.8 | 27.9 | 100 |
| 12 | 18.2 | 12.5 | 18.6 | 6.4 | 16.1 | 28.2 | 100 |
| 13 | 14.3 | 10.0 | 18.7 | 11.2 | 12.4 | 33.5 | 100 |
| 14 | 16.2 | 11.1 | 22.5 | 15.0 | 7.1 | 28.1 | 100 |
| 15 | 14.4 | 14.4 | 21.9 | 18.5 | 4.8 | 25.9 | 100 |
| 16 | 17.9 | 15.1 | 18.6 | 20.2 | 3.2 | 25.0 | 100 |
| 17 | 21.3 | 13.2 | 19.9 | 20.8 | 1.8 | 23.1 | 100 |
| 18 | 19.4 | 13.0 | 20.5 | 24.5 | 1.9 | 20.7 | 100 |
| 19 | 19.9 | 11.4 | 21.9 | 28.0 | 1.4 | 17.5 | 100 |
| National | 14.3 | 10.9 | 11.3 | 7.3 | 37.5 | 18.7 | 100 |

*Source:* NPS 2008, Education History Module.
*Note:* The proportion reflects the average proportion at each age of respondents mentioning that reason for not attending school, over the period 1998–2008.
a. Supply-side problems include no school vacancy, school is too far away, no good school for the level/grade, the school is closed, no teachers, teacher is not dedicated, and lack of books.
b. High cost includes school fee, uniform costs, and material costs.
c. Work includes work outside the home, on the farm, for the household, take care of sick members, and take care of family.
d. Age corresponds to age in the year of not being enrolled. Population excludes those who last attended school before 1998.

**Table A.7  Dropout Rates in EP1 and EP2 (% respondents), 2003 and 2008**

| | 2003 | | 2008 | |
|---|---|---|---|---|
| Population[a] | EP1 | EP2 | EP1 | EP2 |
| Urban | 4.6 | 9.0 | 4.1 | 8.7 |
| Rural | 8.3 | 14.9 | 6.3 | 15.9 |
| Male | 7.7 | 10.7 | 4.9 | 9.9 |
| Female | 6.4 | 12.1 | 6.3 | 13.9 |
| National | 7.1 | 11.2 | 5.6 | 11.8 |

*Sources:* MICS 2008; IAF 2002–03; Poverty and Social Impact Analysis (PSIA) 2005.
a. Calculated as the proportion of people in that year who responded "drop out" to the question of "at the end of the school year did the student…."

**Table A.8  Repetition Rates in EP1 and EP2, by Area of Residence and Gender, 2008**

|  | EP1 | | EP2 | |
| --- | --- | --- | --- | --- |
| Population | Urban (%) | Rural (%) | Urban (%) | Rural (%) |
| Male | 8.4 | 11.5 | 5.9 | 6.7 |
| Female | 8.4 | 12.3 | 5.7 | 5.3 |
| National | 8.4 | 11.9 | 5.8 | 6.2 |

*Source:* MICS 2008.

**Table A.9  Proportion Spent (per student) on Each Type of Cost in EP1 and EP2, by Area of Residence**

|  | EP1 | | EP2 | |
| --- | --- | --- | --- | --- |
| Contribution | Urban (%) | Rural (%) | Urban (%) | Rural (%) |
| Obligatory contribution to school | 9.6 | 7.0 | 8.8 | 9.1 |
| Voluntary contribution to school | 7.5 | 15.9 | 5.7 | 6.5 |
| Material | 61.1 | 66.4 | 70.8 | 74.7 |
| Other | 21.8 | 10.7 | 14.7 | 9.6 |

*Source:* NPS 2008.

**Table A.10  Per Student Education Expenditure (Mt) by Type of Cost and Consumption Quintile, 2008**

| Quintile | Type of cost | EP1 | EP2 | ES1 | ES2[a] |
| --- | --- | --- | --- | --- | --- |
| 1 | Obligatory contribution to school | 4.4 | 32.9 | 99.7 | — |
|  | Voluntary contribution to school | 10.0 | 9.1 | 10.4 | — |
|  | Material | 52.6 | 164.2 | 196.9 | — |
|  | Other expenditures | 4.3 | 10.2 | 26.8 | — |
| 2 | Obligatory contribution to school | 5.6 | 14.7 | 237.2 | — |
|  | Voluntary contribution to school | 13.3 | 12.1 | 15.9 | — |
|  | Material | 66.8 | 156.4 | 536.1 | — |
|  | Other expenditures | 4.8 | 9.8 | 104.3 | — |
| 3 | Obligatory contribution to school | 9.2 | 43.8 | 230.6 | 307.4 |
|  | Voluntary contribution to school | 22.7 | 25.1 | 35.1 | 0.0 |
|  | Material | 89.7 | 378.4 | 543.2 | 722.5 |
|  | Other expenditures | 25.5 | 18.2 | 182.6 | 652.7 |
| 4 | Obligatory contribution to school | 13.6 | 29.9 | 377.0 | 457.9 |
|  | Voluntary contribution to school | 18.1 | 22.8 | 33.5 | 19.5 |

*(continued next page)*

**Table A.10** *(continued)*

| Quintile | Type of cost | EP1 | EP2 | ES1 | ES2[a] |
|---|---|---|---|---|---|
| 5 | Material | 129.8 | 337.6 | 474.3 | 697.2 |
|   | Other expenditures | 18.4 | 63.5 | 278.7 | 854.4 |
|   | Obligatory contribution to school | 50.4 | 61.0 | 326.0 | 2,489.0 |
|   | Voluntary contribution to school | 36.0 | 52.9 | 54.0 | 22.0 |
|   | Material | 220.1 | 376.9 | 636.0 | 789.3 |
|   | Other expenditures | 122.4 | 129.9 | 613.3 | 2,135.1 |
| All | Obligatory contribution to school | 12.4 | 35.7 | 298.9 | 2,039.3 |
|   | Voluntary contribution to school | 17.7 | 24.4 | 38.3 | 19.3 |
|   | Material | 95.9 | 290.4 | 533.3 | 772.5 |
|   | Other expenditures | 24.2 | 48.7 | 362.7 | 1,839.7 |

*Source:* NPS 2008.
*Notes:* Expenditures made by the population ages 6–19 that went to school in the previous year, 2007.
a. Sample sizes are 3, 5, and 26 for ES2 in Quintiles 3, 4, and 5, respectively. Given the very small sample sizes (particularly in Q3 and Q4) the results are not recommended for inference or conclusions.


**Table A.11  Comparison of Annual Per Student Expenditures on Obligatory Contributions (fees), (Mt, constant 2008 prices), 2003 and 2008**

|  | Consumption Quintile | | | | |
|---|---|---|---|---|---|
|  | 1 | 2 | 3 | 4 | 5 |
| 2003 | | | | | |
| EP1 | 25.9 | 27.0 | 27.2 | 31.3 | 67.3 |
| EP2 | 69.9 | 65.3 | 69.0 | 104.8 | 160.7 |
| 2008 | | | | | |
| Obligatory | | | | | |
| EP1 | 4.4 | 5.6 | 9.2 | 13.6 | 50.4 |
| EP2 | 32.9 | 14.7 | 43.8 | 29.9 | 61.0 |
| Voluntary | | | | | |
| EP1 | 10.0 | 13.3 | 22.7 | 18.1 | 36.0 |
| EP2 | 9.1 | 12.1 | 25.1 | 22.8 | 52.9 |
| Total fees (O + V) | | | | | |
| EP1 | 14.4 | 18.9 | 31.9 | 31.7 | 86.4 |
| EP2 | 42.0 | 26.8 | 68.9 | 52.7 | 113.9 |

*Sources:* IAF 2002–03; World Bank 2005; NPS 2008. In 2008, fees were set at the local level and are labeled "obligatory" if households identified them as such.
*Note:* 2008 is the base year. To calculate other years' price indices, the series of average consumer data for 2000–10 (base 2000) from IMF was used.

### Table A.12  Perceptions of Change in Quality of Education since 2004 (% households), by Consumption Quintile

| Compared to 2004, education quality… | 1 | 2 | 3 | 4 | 5 | National |
|---|---|---|---|---|---|---|
| Improved | 79.7 | 85.3 | 88.7 | 77.4 | 71.9 | 81.5 |
| Is the same | 18.3 | 10.0 | 6.5 | 10.0 | 12.9 | 11.6 |
| Worsened | 2.0 | 4.6 | 4.8 | 12.6 | 15.2 | 6.9 |
| Total | 100 | 100 | 100 | 100 | 100 | 100 |

*Source:* NPS 2008.
*Note:* Estimates are based on all who answered this question, regardless of whether they were sending or not sending their kids to school. Results are very similar if only households with children in school are used.

### Table A.13  Main Reason for Education Improvement (% households citing reason), 2008

| Reason | 1 | 2 | 3 | 4 | 5 | National |
|---|---|---|---|---|---|---|
| Expansion of school system | 12.2 | 7.6 | 11.7 | 10.6 | 20.5 | 11.6 |
| Increase in number of teachers | 4.8 | 3.0 | 2.6 | 5.3 | 5.7 | 4.0 |
| Improved quality of curriculum | 3.1 | 2.5 | 5.8 | 5.2 | 3.0 | 3.9 |
| Free school material | 13.9 | 26.0 | 13.8 | 22.0 | 12.0 | 18.2 |
| Free books | 16.6 | 13.5 | 21.1 | 13.3 | 11.2 | 15.6 |
| Abolition of school fees | 49.5 | 46.6 | 44.4 | 43.1 | 46.9 | 46.2 |
| Other | 0.0 | 0.8 | 0.6 | 0.5 | 0.7 | 0.5 |
| Total | 100 | 100 | 100 | 100 | 100 | 100 |

*Source:* NPS 2008.
*Note:* Among those who mentioned that education had "improved" after the results, these were the main reasons given for improvement of the system.

### Table A.14  Main Reason for Education Worsening (% households citing reason), 2008

| | 1 | 2 | 3 | 4 | 5 | National |
|---|---|---|---|---|---|---|
| Lack of schools | 21.4 | 8.5 | 2.2 | 5.5 | 3.8 | 6.1 |
| School is too far away | 0.6 | 0.0 | 5.5 | 0.0 | 6.3 | 2.7 |
| Lack of teachers | 12.4 | 4.5 | 0.0 | 0.0 | 0.9 | 1.8 |
| Lack of desks | 0.0 | 14.0 | 0.0 | 0.9 | 0.0 | 2.6 |
| Corruption | 15.9 | 8.9 | 19.8 | 7.6 | 8.1 | 10.3 |
| Change in curriculum | 42.6 | 57.8 | 39.2 | 33.7 | 61.2 | 47.2 |
| Annexed classrooms | 0.0 | 0.0 | 0.0 | 1.1 | 0.0 | 0.4 |
| Other | 7.0 | 6.3 | 33.4 | 51.1 | 19.6 | 29.0 |
| Total | 100.0 | 100.0 | 100.0 | 100.0 | 100.0 | 100.0 |

*Source:* NPS 2008.
*Note:* Among those who mentioned that education had "worsened" after the results, these were the main reasons given for worsening of the system.

## Secondary Education: Enrollment Rates and School Expenditures

**Table A.15 Gross Enrollment Rates in Secondary, by Area of Residence and Gender, 1997, 2003, 2008 (% of population)**

|  | Urban | | Rural | | |
| --- | --- | --- | --- | --- | --- |
| Level/year | Male | Female | Male | Female | National |
| ES1 |  |  |  |  |  |
| 1997 | 27.5 | 27.3 | 3.5 | 1.2 | 8.5 |
| 2003 | 63.7 | 49.4 | 4.1 | 2.2 | 22.8 |
| 2008 | 86.8 | 75.1 | 24.6 | 16.1 | 41.9 |
| ES2 |  |  |  |  |  |
| 1997 | 20.5 | 8.6 | 0.4 | 0.0 | 3.8 |
| 2003 | 22.1 | 14.4 | n.a. | 0.3 | 7.9 |
| 2008 | 39.4 | 25.2 | 20.9 | 12.2 | 16.6 |

*Sources:* MICS 2008; IAF 2002–03; IAF 1996–97.
*Note:* The age groups used in this table are the ones used prior to the 2006 change: 14–16 in ES1 and 17–18 in ES2. n.a. = not available.

**Table A.16 Net Enrollment Rates in Secondary, by Area of Residence and Gender, 1997, 2003, 2008 (% of population)**

| Level/year | Rural | Urban | Male | Female | National |
| --- | --- | --- | --- | --- | --- |
| ES1 |  |  |  |  |  |
| 1997 | 0.8 | 9.6 | 2.8 | 3.0 | 2.9 |
| 2003 | 0.6 | 13.9 | 5.1 | 5.9 | 5.5 |
| 2008 | 4.3 | 20.9 | 9.1 | 11.3 | 10.2 |
| ES2 |  |  |  |  |  |
| 1997 | 0.0 | 2.5 | 0.9 | 0.4 | 0.6 |
| 2003 | 0.1 | 2.9 | 1.7 | 0.7 | 1.2 |
| 2008 | 0.6 | 4.8 | 1.8 | 3.1 | 2.4 |

*Sources:* MICS 2008, IAF 2002–03, IAF 1996–97
*Note:* The age groups used in this table are the ones used prior to the 2006 change: 14–16 in ES1 and 17–18 in ES2.

**Table A.17 Dropout Rates in ES1 and ES2, by Area of Residence and Gender, 2008 (% of population)**

|  | ES1 | | ES2 | |
| --- | --- | --- | --- | --- |
| Gender | Urban | Rural | Urban | Rural |
| Male | 5.3 | 13.2 | 16.0 | 23.5 |
| Female | 9.2 | 17.6 | 18.3 | n.a. |

*Source:* MICS 2008.
*Note:* n.a. = not available.

**Table A.18 Educational Expenditure (Mt/student/year) in ES1, by Consumption Quintile, 2008**

| Type of cost | 1 | 2 | 3 | 4 | 5 |
|---|---|---|---|---|---|
| Obligatory contribution to school | 99.7 | 237.2 | 230.6 | 377.0 | 326.0 |
| Voluntary contribution to school | 10.4 | 15.9 | 35.1 | 33.5 | 54.0 |
| Material | 196.9 | 536.1 | 543.2 | 474.3 | 636.0 |
| Other | 26.8 | 104.3 | 182.6 | 278.7 | 613.3 |

Source: NPS 2008.
Note: Since the sample size by quintile in ES2 is extremely small, these numbers are not reported.

**Table A.19 Per Student Annual Expenditure (Mt) in ES1, by Area of Residence and Type of Expenditure**

| Expenditure type | Urban | Rural |
|---|---|---|
| Obligatory contribution to school | 356.1 | 225.2 |
| Voluntary contribution to school | 34.1 | 43.8 |
| Material | 582.4 | 470.1 |
| Other expenditures | 464.8 | 231.1 |
| Total | 1,437.4 | 970.2 |

Source: NPS 2008.
Note: "Other" includes transportation, boarding, school snack, tutor, documents and copies, and other student expenses. Since the sample size by quintile in ES2 is extremely small, these numbers are not reported.

**Table A.20  Share of the Labor Force (%) with Primary Education, 2003, 2008, and Projected for 2013**

| Age group | | % in 2003 | % in 2008 | Test 2003 = 08 | % in 2013 | Test 2008 = 13 | Test 2003 = 13 |
|---|---|---|---|---|---|---|---|
| *Less than complete EP1* | | | | | | | |
| 20–64 | | 69.1 | 66.6 | | 66.4 | | |
| | s.e. | 2.3 | 2.2 | | 2.4 | | |
| 20–24 | | 76.5 | 75.2 | | 77.4 | | |
| | s.e. | 3.5 | 4.2 | | 4.7 | | |
| 25–29 | | 71.1 | 75.5 | | 77.1 | | |
| | s.e. | 3.2 | 3.7 | | 3.9 | | |
| 30–34 | | 73.9 | 62.6 | ** | 70.1 | * | |
| | s.e. | 3.9 | 4.6 | | 3.0 | | |
| 35–39 | | 77.8 | 72.0 | | 59.2 | *** | *** |
| | s.e. | 3.7 | 4.0 | | 3.8 | | |
| 40–44 | | 73.9 | 65.5 | | 65.7 | | |
| | s.e. | 4.3 | 4.5 | | 3.7 | | |
| 45–49 | | 57.0 | 60.5 | | 59.6 | | |
| | s.e. | 5.2 | 6.3 | | 3.4 | | |
| 50–54 | | 57.7 | 54.8 | | 58.1 | | |
| | s.e. | 6.4 | 5.0 | | 4.9 | | |
| 55–59 | | 60.4 | 58.2 | | 52.9 | | |
| | s.e. | 8.0 | 5.9 | | 3.4 | | |
| 60–64 | | 26.0 | 49.6 | * | 52.2 | | *** |
| | s.e. | 9.4 | 9.8 | | 4.1 | | |
| *Primary 1 complete* | | | | | | | |
| 20–64 | | 21.0 | 29.1 | *** | 35.2 | *** | *** |
| | s.e. | 2.1 | 2.6 | | 2.8 | | |
| 20–24 | | 23.2 | 44.9 | *** | 52.1 | | *** |
| | s.e. | 3.6 | 5.5 | | 5.3 | | |
| 25–29 | | 18.2 | 39.6 | *** | 52.7 | ** | *** |
| | s.e. | 2.9 | 5.3 | | 5.3 | | |
| 30–34 | | 25.9 | 24.2 | | 38.0 | *** | ** |
| | s.e. | 4.1 | 4.3 | | 4.3 | | |
| 35–39 | | 23.9 | 34.1 | * | 24.1 | * | |
| | s.e. | 3.8 | 4.9 | | 3.8 | | |
| 40–44 | | 22.4 | 21.6 | | 33.4 | ** | ** |
| | s.e. | 3.6 | 4.0 | | 4.6 | | |
| 45–49 | | 21.7 | 25.3 | | 22.6 | | |
| | s.e. | 3.6 | 5.9 | | 3.5 | | |
| 50–54 | | 17.5 | 16.4 | | 25.7 | | |
| | s.e. | 4.6 | 3.5 | | 5.5 | | |
| 55–59 | | 12.9 | 12.4 | | 18.6 | | |
| | s.e. | 3.7 | 3.9 | | 3.0 | | |
| 60–64 | | 7.2 | 14.8 | | 14.6 | | * |
| | s.e. | 3.2 | 8.5 | | 3.2 | | |

*(continued next page)*

**Table A.20** (continued)

| Age group | | % in 2003 | % in 2008 | Test 2003 = 08 | % in 2013 | Test 2008 = 13 | Test 2003 = 13 |
|---|---|---|---|---|---|---|---|
| *Primary 2 complete* | | | | | | | |
| 20–64 | | 8.9 | 17.9 | *** | 25.2 | *** | *** |
| | s.e. | 1.2 | 2.1 | | 2.5 | | |
| 20–24 | | 6.7 | 28.6 | *** | 40.3 | * | *** |
| | s.e. | 1.6 | 5.5 | | 5.3 | | |
| 25–29 | | 8.6 | 24.0 | *** | 43.0 | *** | *** |
| | s.e. | 1.8 | 4.0 | | 5.3 | | |
| 30–34 | | 11.2 | 13.6 | | 25.7 | *** | *** |
| | s.e. | 2.3 | 3.1 | | 3.6 | | |
| 35–39 | | 11.1 | 25.6 | *** | 15.0 | ** | |
| | s.e. | 2.3 | 5.2 | | 3.0 | | |
| 40–44 | | 9.8 | 10.2 | | 22.9 | *** | *** |
| | s.e. | 2.2 | 2.8 | | 4.2 | | |
| 45–49 | | 10.7 | 17.5 | | 13.0 | | |
| | s.e. | 2.8 | 6.1 | | 2.7 | | |
| 50–54 | | 8.5 | 10.1 | | 17.2 | | * |
| | s.e. | 2.9 | 2.6 | | 4.5 | | |
| 55–59 | | 3.3 | 5.8 | | 11.3 | * | *** |
| | s.e. | 1.9 | 2.3 | | 2.5 | | |
| 60–64 | | n.a. | 0.9 | | 7.7 | *** | *** |
| | s.e. | n.a. | 0.7 | | 2.3 | | |

*Source:* Authors' calculations.
*Note:* Inverse probability weighting. The sample for 2003 includes the individuals surveyed in 2003 and 2008. All the workers ages 20–64 are included in the sample. The standard errors of the estimators are corrected for the correlation between the different observations in the same enumeration area and computed by bootstrap with 1,000 replications. n.a. = not available, s.e. = standard error.
***$p < 0.01$, **$p < 0.05$, *$p < 0.1$.

**Table A.21  Share of the Labor Force (%) with Secondary Education, 2003, 2008, and Projected for 2013**

| Age group | | % in 2003 | % in 2008 | Test 2003 = 08 | % in 2013 | Test 2008 = 13 | Test 2003 = 13 |
|---|---|---|---|---|---|---|---|
| *Secondary 1 complete* | | | | | | | |
| 20–64 | | 3.2 | 5.8 | *** | 9.1 | *** | *** |
| | s.e. | 0.6 | 1.2 | | 1.7 | | |
| 20–24 | | 1.5 | 3.6 | | 10.8 | ** | *** |
| | s.e. | 0.8 | 1.8 | | 3.6 | | |
| 25–29 | | 2.4 | 12.3 | *** | 21.0 | ** | *** |
| | s.e. | 0.9 | 3.6 | | 5.7 | | |
| 30–34 | | 3.8 | 4.4 | | 10.3 | ** | ** |
| | s.e. | 1.2 | 1.5 | | 2.8 | | |
| 35–39 | | 5.3 | 6.0 | | 5.4 | | |
| | s.e. | 1.6 | 1.9 | | 1.6 | | |
| 40–44 | | 4.4 | 4.9 | | 6.6 | | |
| | s.e. | 1.4 | 1.7 | | 1.8 | | |
| 45–49 | | 4.3 | 5.7 | | 4.6 | | |
| | s.e. | 1.5 | 2.6 | | 1.4 | | |
| 50–54 | | 2.0 | 4.7 | | 5.8 | | |
| | s.e. | 1.2 | 2.1 | | 2.2 | | |
| 55–59 | | n.a. | 3.2 | * | 3.7 | | *** |
| | s.e. | | 1.9 | | 1.5 | | |
| 60–64 | | n.a. | 0.2 | | 2.1 | | * |
| | s.e. | | 0.2 | | 1.2 | | |
| *Secondary 2 complete* | | | | | | | |
| 20–64 | | 1.0 | 2.0 | *** | 3.6 | *** | *** |
| | s.e. | 0.3 | 0.6 | | 1.0 | | |
| 20–24 | | n.a. | 0.0 | | 4.0 | * | * |
| | s.e. | | 0.7 | | 2.2 | | |
| 25–29 | | 0.3 | 3.0 | ** | 5.0 | | |
| | s.e. | 0.2 | 1.2 | | 3.0 | | |
| 30–34 | | 1.1 | 2.5 | | 5.7 | | |
| | s.e. | 0.6 | 1.3 | | 2.1 | | |
| 35–39 | | 2.3 | 2.8 | | 3.1 | | |
| | s.e. | 0.9 | 1.2 | | 1.3 | | |
| 40–44 | | 2.6 | 2.2 | | 2.9 | | |
| | s.e. | 1.0 | 0.9 | | 1.1 | | |
| 45–49 | | 0.9 | 3.1 | | 2.3 | | |
| | s.e. | 0.6 | 1.7 | | 0.8 | | * |
| 50–54 | | n.a. | 1.5 | | 2.9 | | |
| | s.e. | | 1.1 | | 1.4 | | ** |
| 55–59 | | n.a. | 0.5 | | 1.7 | | |
| | s.e. | | 0.5 | | 0.9 | | * |
| 60–64 | | n.a. | 0.2 | | 0.9 | | |
| | s.e. | | 0.2 | | 0.6 | | |

*Source:* Authors' calculations.
*Note:* Inverse probability weighting. The sample for 2003 includes the individuals surveyed in 2003 and 2008. All the workers ages 20-64 are included in the sample. The standard errors of the estimators are corrected for the correlation between the different observations in the same enumeration area and computed by bootstrap with 1,000 replications. n.a. = not available, s.e. = standard error.
***p < 0.01, **p < 0.05, *p < 0.1.

**Table A.22  Share of the Labor Force with Education, 2003, 2008, and Alternative Projections for 2013**

| Share of active population with: | | 2003 (%) | 2008 (%) | 2013 (%) | Test 2013 = 2003 | Test 2013 = 2008 | 2013, double primary transition rates (%) | Test: 2013, double primary transition rates = 2003 | Test: 2013, double primary transition rates = 2008 | 2013, double secondary transition rates (%) | Test: 2013, double secondary transition rates = 2003 | Test: 2013, double secondary transition rates = 2008 |
|---|---|---|---|---|---|---|---|---|---|---|---|---|
| Less than complete EP1 | | 69.1 | 66.6 | 66.4 | | | 67.2 | | | 66.4 | | |
| | s.e. | 2.2 | 2.2 | 2.4 | | | 2.4 | | | 2.4 | | |
| Primary 1 | | 28.2 | 31.3 | 35.2 | *** | *** | 36.9 | *** | *** | 35.2 | *** | *** |
| | s.e. | 2.9 | 2.6 | 2.7 | | | 2.8 | | | 2.7 | | |
| Primary 2 | | 12.4 | 19.2 | 25.2 | *** | *** | 28.0 | *** | *** | 25.2 | *** | *** |
| | s.e. | 1.7 | 2.1 | 2.3 | | | 2.5 | | | 2.3 | | |
| Secondary 1 | | 4.9 | 6.0 | 9.1 | *** | *** | 9.7 | *** | *** | 10.3 | *** | *** |
| | s.e. | 1.0 | 1.1 | 1.5 | | | 1.5 | | | 1.7 | | |
| Secondary 2 | | 1.7 | 2.3 | 3.6 | ** | * | 3.7 | ** | * | 4.6 | *** | ** |
| | s.e. | 0.5 | 0.5 | 1.0 | | | 1.1 | | | 1.3 | | |

*Sources:* NPS 2008 and IAF 2003.

*Note:* Inverse probability weighting. The sample for 2003 includes the individuals surveyed in 2003 and 2008. Labor force is ages 20–64. The standard errors of the estimators are corrected for the correlation between the different observations in the same enumeration area and computed by bootstrap with 1,000 replications. s.e. = standard error.
*** $p < 0.01$, ** $p < 0.05$, * $p < 0.1$.

## APPENDIX B

# Simulation of Enrollment Rate Scenarios

This appendix describes the method used to compute the projected education survival rates and the potential qualifications of future labor shown in figures 6.1 and 6.2. In computing these estimates, we used the NPS data. We did not start with a demographic model, so we did not estimate deaths and withdrawals from the labor force by education and age. Instead, we only projected the labor force for prime working age: 20–60, separately for males and females. We found that this simple simulation nonetheless provided a very clear picture of the tradeoffs Mozambique faces.

In addition, the sampling method used in the NPS was designed to get a random sample of children, not households. As a result, the panel data do not represent a random sample of Mozambique's labor force in 2008. However, we still expect them to indicate the direction of the change.

### Main Simulation

The main simulation is based on a very simple hypothesis: Let $a$ be an age group (group $a$ could be individuals ages 15–19, 20–24, 25–29, etc.). $a_t$ groups all the individuals of the age group $a$ at date $t$. Group $a_t$ is divided into workers and non-workers ($w_t=1$ or $w_t=0$); people have education $e_t$. Using our panel data information on the education, work, and

89

age status in 2008 given the education, age, and work in 2003, we estimate the following probabilities:

$$\begin{cases} P(w_{2008}=1|w_{2003},e_{2003},a_{2003}) \\ P(e_{2008}>l|w_{2008},w_{2003},e_{2003},a_{2003}) \end{cases}$$

Our simulation makes the simple hypothesis:

$$\begin{cases} P(w_{2013}=1|w_{2008},e_{2008},a_{2008})=P(w_{2008}=1|w_{2003},e_{2003},a_{2003}) \\ P(e_{2013}>l|w_{2013},w_{2008},e_{2008},a_{2008})=P(e_{2008}>l|w_{2008},w_{2003},e_{2003},a_{2003}) \end{cases}$$

Hence we induce the probability that an individual has a given education in 2013 if he or she works and $P(e_{2013}>l|w_{2013},w_{2008},e_{2008},a_{2008})$ (and the probability that he actually works).

The average of this probability over the sample gives the education of the labor force in 2013.

## Standard Errors

The standard errors of the estimators are computed by bootstrap with 1,000 replications. They are corrected for the correlation between the different observations in the same enumeration area: the bootstrap computation is done enumeration area by enumeration area. This procedure computes standard errors based on the effect of random sampling on the precision of (1) the share of educated people in the sample and (2) the transition probabilities computed.

Hence these standard errors do not reflect possible changes in behavior, which would make the probabilities inferred in 2003–08 irrelevant for 2008–13.

## Simulation with Double Transition Rates

This section describes the procedure used to estimate the change in the projected qualifications of the labor force if the transition rates doubled (the estimates shown in figure 6.2). The basic idea is to multiply the probability that human capital increases for an individual by 2.

$$\tilde{P}(e^*_{2013}=h|w_{2013},w_{2008},e^*_{2008}=l,a_{2008})$$
$$=2P(e^*_{2008}=h|w_{2008},w_{2003},e^*_{2003}=l,a_{2003}) \text{ if } h:$$

Again, we have a problem with measurement error. A part in the increase in education is matched by a decrease in education, and hence presumably due to noise. On the other hand, we multiply by 2 the increase that is not matched by a decrease in education, and probably not due to noise:

if $h > l$ and $P(e_{2008} = h, w_{2008}, w_{2003}, e_{2003} = l, a_{2003})$
$> P(e_{2008} = l, w_{2008}, w_{2003}, e_{2003} = h, a_{2003})$

$P(e_{2013} = h, w_{2013}, w_{2008}, e_{2008} = l, a_{2003})$
$= P(e_{2008} = l, w_{2008}, w_{2003}, e_{2003} = h, a_{2003})$
$+ 2[P(e_{2008} = h, w_{2008}, w_{2003}, e_{2003} = l, a_{2003})$
$- P(e_{2008} = l, w_{2008}, w_{2003}, e_{2003} = h, a_{2003})]$
$= P(e_{2008} = h, w_{2008}, w_{2003}, e_{2003} = l, a_{2003})$
$- [P(e_{2008} = l, w_{2008}, w_{2003}, e_{2003} = h, a_{2003})$
$- P(e_{2008} = h, w_{2008}, w_{2003}, e_{2003} = l, a_{2003})]$

When there is no reason to suspect an increase in "real" education, we do not multiply any probability by 2:

if $h < l$ or $P(e_{2008} = h, w_{2008}, w_{2003}, e_{2003} = l, a_{2003})$
$\leq P(e_{2008} = l, w_{2008}, w_{2003}, e_{2003} = h, a_{2003})$

$\tilde{P}(e_{2013} = h, w_{2013}, w_{2008}, e_{2008} = l, a_{2008})$
$= P(e_{2008} = h, w_{2008}, w_{2003}, e_{2003} = l, a_{2003})$

We have multiplied by 2 the probability that education increases. We compute the total effect of the multiplication of the probability that education increases:

*Sum*

$= \sum_{h \neq l} \tilde{P}(e_{2013} = h, w_{2013}, w_{2008}, e_{2008} = l, a_{2008})$
$\quad - P(e_{2008} = h, w_{2008}, w_{2003}, e_{2003} = l, a_{2003})$
$= \sum_{h \neq l} \max(P(e_{2008} = h, w_{2008}, w_{2003}, e_{2003} = l, a_{2003})$
$\quad - P(e_{2008} = l, w_{2008}, w_{2003}, e_{2003} = h, a_{2003}), 0)$

And this is subtracted from the probability that education remains the same:

$$\tilde{P}(e_{2008} = h, w_{2013}, w_{2008}, e_{2008} = h, a_{2008})$$
$$= P(e_{2008} = h, w_{2013}, w_{2008}, e_{2008} = h, a_{2008}) - Sum$$

However, this generates a problem when $P(e_{2008} = h, w_{2013}, w_{2008}, e_{2008} = h, a_{2008}) - Sum$. In these cases: $\tilde{P}(e_{2008} = h, w_{2013}, w_{2008}, e_{2008} = h, a_{2008}) = 0$, $Su$ and we cannot increase education so much. Then the increase in education in each case is proportional to its contribution to *sum*.

In the end, the sum of $\tilde{P}(e_{2008} = h, w_{2013}, w_{2008}, e_{2008} = h, a_{2008})$ over all the sample simulates the education of the labor force in 2013.

## APPENDIX C

# Econometric Estimation of the Program Effect

This appendix summarizes the basic model and results of the econometric estimate of the effect of the 2004–05 reform program on primary school enrollment.

### The Basic Model: Effect of the Program for the Exposed Group

We adopt the method of Duflo (2001) that uses time and ages of the child to identify the effect of the program. The panel data from the Education History Module of NPS 2008 provides us the information on enrollment status with the level of education of each individual in each year from 1998 to 2008. Since enrollment is relevant only for the group of people within the school ages 6 to 19,[1] we estimate an equation based on an unbalanced panel data of individuals ages 6–19 in the year that their school attendance was asked. The panel data is unbalanced since not all individuals were observed throughout all 10 years. If the child was between ages 6 and 9 in 1998, she or he will be observed in every year between 1998 and 2008. If they were older than 9 in 1998, they would be included until they became 19 but not in the later years when they age above 19 or become too old for primary school. Similarly, young children who were too young (younger than 6) to go to school are not included in the initial years but will join the selected sample later as they turn 6.

Since the program removed the tuition, thus lowering the cost to all children in primary school, it affects the decision making on whether to send children between the ages of 6 and 12 (the official primary school age) to school, presuming that children start school at age 6. Children 13 years or older are likely to complete primary school and either advance to secondary school or drop out due to higher costs of secondary school. Their decisions to attend secondary school should not be affected by abolishing fees in primary education. Therefore, we identify ages 6 to 12 (the age in the year of enrollment) as the treatment group, the group that were exposed to the program since the implementation of the program in 2005, and the control group is ages 13–19. We estimate a difference-in-differences equation:

$$S_{it} = \alpha + \beta_1 Y05_t + \gamma T_{it} + \delta(Y05_t{}^*T_{it}) + \beta_2 X_i + u_{it}, \qquad (1)$$

where $S_{it}$ is a dummy variable equal to one if the child is enrolled in school in year t and zero otherwise; $\alpha$ is a constant; $Y05_t$ indicates the post program period (a dummy variable equal to 1 from year 2005 and after and 0 for the years before); $T_{it}$ is equal to one if child $i$ is ages 6–12 in year $t$; $X_i$ contains the 2008 characteristics of children (gender); household (rural, female headed, parental education, the absence and death of mother and father, household per capita consumption); characteristics of the district (district average travel time to school [minutes], district average per capita consumption), and provincial fixed effects; and the error term $u_{it}$.[2] All models are estimated with the probit model for the whole population ages 6–19 and separately for urban and rural, males and females. The parameter $\beta_1$ measures the increase in enrollment of all ages after 2005 that can be implied by improvements in the aggregate condition, and $\delta$ captures the effect of the program on the treatment group. Given our identification strategy, $\delta$ is the difference over time in the average difference of enrollment rates of primary-school-age (6–12 years old) children and higher-than-primary-school-age (13–19 years old) children.

Table C1 displays the marginal effects of our variables of interest based on equation 1, including the treatment group, the year effect, and the program effect, which is the coefficients on the interaction term for the whole sample, urban and rural, males and females ages 6–19. The positive and statistically significant coefficients on the interaction terms

**Table C.1  Effect of the Program for the Exposed Group, Population Ages 6–19 Years**

| Variables | (1) All | (2) Urban | (3) Rural | (4) Male | (5) Female |
|---|---|---|---|---|---|
| Treatment group (ages 6–12) | −0.0923*** | −0.0572*** | −0.125*** | −0.122*** | −0.0697*** |
|  | (0.00912) | (0.0103) | (0.0145) | (0.0118) | (0.0142) |
| Post-program years (from 2005 and after) | 0.163*** | 0.112*** | 0.188*** | 0.150*** | 0.166*** |
|  | (0.0102) | (0.0116) | (0.0155) | (0.0138) | (0.0153) |
| Treatment group post-program * | 0.116*** | 0.0876*** | 0.132*** | 0.114*** | 0.131*** |
|  | (0.0120) | (0.0138) | (0.0185) | (0.0161) | (0.0180) |
| Female | −0.0531*** | −0.0395*** | −0.0595*** |  |  |
|  | (0.00612) | (0.00757) | (0.00875) |  |  |
| Rural | −0.119*** |  |  | −0.134*** | −0.0772*** |
|  | (0.0103) |  |  | (0.0134) | (0.0166) |
| Female headed household | 0.0459*** | 0.0661*** | 0.0251** | 0.0394*** | 0.0473*** |
|  | (0.00832) | (0.00990) | (0.0122) | (0.0116) | (0.0122) |
| Log of per capita consumption | 0.0775*** | 0.0853*** | 0.0637*** | 0.0652*** | 0.0918*** |
|  | (0.00430) | (0.00546) | (0.00614) | (0.00585) | (0.00646) |
| *Mother's education* |  |  |  |  |  |
| Alphabetization | 0.0493** | −0.0389 | 0.109*** | 0.0644** | 0.0352 |
|  | (0.0243) | (0.0332) | (0.0367) | (0.0316) | (0.0373) |
| EP1 | 0.0712*** | 0.0627*** | 0.0524* | 0.0282* | 0.120*** |
|  | (0.0121) | (0.0110) | (0.0290) | (0.0170) | (0.0174) |
| EP2 | 0.123*** | 0.0585*** | 0.238*** | 0.0859*** | 0.169*** |
|  | (0.0154) | (0.0150) | (0.0319) | (0.0211) | (0.0223) |
| ES1 or higher | 0.204*** | 0.125*** | 0.356*** | 0.195*** | 0.222*** |
|  | (0.0209) | (0.0178) | (0.0532) | (0.0266) | (0.0320) |
| Mother absent | −0.0130 | −0.0239 | −0.00748 | −0.00970 | −0.00860 |
|  | (0.0116) | (0.0158) | (0.0156) | (0.0156) | (0.0173) |
| Mother died | −0.0663*** | −0.0688*** | −0.0895*** | −0.0840*** | −0.0369* |
|  | (0.0145) | (0.0192) | (0.0199) | (0.0210) | (0.0202) |
| *Father's education* |  |  |  |  |  |
| Alphabetization | 0.0168 | 0.227*** | −0.191*** | 0.0223 | 0.0485 |
|  | (0.0433) | (0.00838) | (0.0521) | (0.0543) | (0.0687) |
| EP1 | 0.0478*** | 0.0628*** | 0.0246 | 0.0473*** | 0.0536*** |
|  | (0.0113) | (0.0134) | (0.0163) | (0.0145) | (0.0178) |
| EP2 | 0.0608*** | 0.0517*** | 0.0931*** | 0.106*** | −0.00464 |
|  | (0.0132) | (0.0130) | (0.0261) | (0.0154) | (0.0226) |
| ES1 or higher | 0.0645*** | 0.0629*** | 0.100* | 0.0739*** | 0.0524* |
|  | (0.0195) | (0.0168) | (0.0532) | (0.0260) | (0.0292) |
| Father absent | −0.0270** | −0.0103 | −0.0195 | −0.0136 | −0.0422** |
|  | (0.0122) | (0.0167) | (0.0161) | (0.0165) | (0.0181) |
| Father died | −0.0119 | −0.0217 | 0.00997 | 0.0125 | −0.0450** |
|  | (0.0117) | (0.0157) | (0.0160) | (0.0150) | (0.0183) |

*(continued next page)*

**Table C.1**  (continued)

| Variables | (1)<br>All | (2)<br>Urban | (3)<br>Rural | (4)<br>Male | (5)<br>Female |
|---|---|---|---|---|---|
| District average travel time to school | −0.000474*<br>(0.000254) | 0.00165***<br>(0.000483) | −0.00200***<br>(0.000338) | −0.000912***<br>(0.000343) | −0.000132<br>(0.000380) |
| District average consumption (log) | 0.0511***<br>(0.0105) | 0.0813***<br>(0.0200) | 0.00234<br>(0.0149) | 0.00544<br>(0.0139) | 0.114***<br>(0.0162) |
| Observations | 29,044 | 13,674 | 15,370 | 14,834 | 14,210 |
| Pseudo R-squared | 0.155 | 0.117 | 0.130 | 0.135 | 0.185 |

*Source:* NPS 2008.
*Note:* Provincial dummies were included but not presented here. The referenced categories are no education for mother and father. Standard errors in parentheses.
*** $p < 0.01$, ** $p < 0.05$, * $p < 0.1$.

suggest larger increases in enrollment over time for the age group 6–12 compared to that of the 13–19 year olds. Assuming that children no longer attend primary school by age 13, this difference between the two age groups and over time represents the effect of the program on enrollment. The effects are estimated to be 11.6 percent for the whole population ages 6–19, and larger for rural areas (13.2 as opposed to 8.7 percent for urban) and for girls (13.1 percent as opposed to 11.4 percent for boys). This implies that, in addition to the positive effects on the overall population, the program has specifically increased access to education for the poor in rural areas and girls.

This interpretation relies on the assumption that there were no other government measures that also promoted education during the period 2005–08. In the presence of other programs, the effect would be overestimated. Second, the identification strategy is violated if the program also induces more attendance in secondary schools by increasing access to primary education. This spillover effect would be captured in the post-program-year effects and the coefficient on the interaction would underestimate the real effect of the program. Third, the effect is underestimated if there is a sizeable number of late entrants who remain in primary school after age 12. Some older children, due to grade repetition and delayed school entry, might also benefit from the program during their last year in school. Statistics from NPS 2008 show about 26 percent and 15 percent of children ages 13–19 were still in EP1 and EP2, respectively. In addition, the intensity of the treatment varies within the age group 6–12. Younger children starting primary school can benefit more from free primary education than those at the finishing stage after the implementation of the program. To address the last two issues, we present in the next section a model that relaxes the definition of a treatment group and allows for the effects of a program to vary by age.

## The Extended Model: Effect of the Program for Each Age

To allow for the variation of treatment intensity over ages, we estimate the following model that includes all 14 age dummies (ages 6–19) with the age 19 omitted instead of one dummy variable for the exposed age group. The equation is specified as:

$$S_{it} = \alpha + \beta_1 Y05_t + \sum_{l=2}^{14} \gamma_l d_{il} + \sum_{l=2}^{14} \delta_l (Y05_t * d_{il}) + \beta_2 X_i + u_{it}, \quad (2)$$

where $d_{il}$ is a dummy equal to one if the child is age $l$ in year t (age in the year of enrollment). $\delta_l$ measures the effect of the program age $l$ referenced to the omitted program effect of age 19. Children age 6 after the program are likely to fully benefit from all 7 years of free primary schooling, therefore, enrollment should increase the most for this age group. The potential benefits from free primary education decrease as children become older, thus $\delta$ is expected to be decreasing with age and will fade out after age 12.

The results are displayed in table C2. Age shows a quadratic effect on enrollment, with the highest probability of enrollment occurring at age 13. Similar to the results from the basic model, post-program-year effects are positive and statistically significant, suggesting that enrollment increases for all ages after 2005. The increase is also substantially larger for rural areas and girls as observed in the basic model. Figure 4.1 plots the marginal effects of ages on enrollment for before and after the program in 2005 based on estimates of the whole population ages 6–19. The differences between the two curves (the shaded area) are the coefficients on the interaction term, which measure the effect of the program for a given age.

Figure 4.1 shows that the program shifted the distribution of enrollment over ages upward after 2005. The effects of the program are positive and statistically significant for ages 6–12 (table C2, column 1). They also display a pattern of a hump-shaped curve over ages 6–12 with the peak at age 9 and decaying thereafter. The reason why the largest effect does not occur at age 6, according to our hypothesis, is that many children do not start school until age 9. While the positive effects on ages 6–8 suggest

**Table C.2  Effect of the Program for Each Age, Population 6–19 Years**

| Variables | (1) All | (2) Urban | (3) Rural | (4) Male | (5) Female |
|---|---|---|---|---|---|
| Age 6 | −0.232*** | −0.231*** | −0.168*** | −0.305*** | −0.163*** |
|  | (0.0261) | (0.0335) | (0.0416) | (0.0357) | (0.0388) |
| Age 7 | −0.0319 | −0.0524* | 0.0351 | −0.0943*** | 0.0286 |
|  | (0.0249) | (0.0278) | (0.0434) | (0.0350) | (0.0365) |
| Age 8 | 0.0890*** | 0.0610*** | 0.146*** | 0.0408 | 0.136*** |
|  | (0.0219) | (0.0210) | (0.0412) | (0.0307) | (0.0322) |
| Age 9 | 0.156*** | 0.111*** | 0.217*** | 0.107*** | 0.205*** |
|  | (0.0197) | (0.0173) | (0.0389) | (0.0278) | (0.0286) |
| Age 10 | 0.217*** | 0.154*** | 0.291*** | 0.180*** | 0.255*** |
|  | (0.0169) | (0.0137) | (0.0350) | (0.0234) | (0.0251) |
| Age 11 | 0.261*** | 0.180*** | 0.350*** | 0.223*** | 0.300*** |
|  | (0.0145) | (0.0112) | (0.0309) | (0.0203) | (0.0214) |
| Age 12 | 0.270*** | 0.169*** | 0.388*** | 0.231*** | 0.313*** |
|  | (0.0139) | (0.0120) | (0.0276) | (0.0196) | (0.0199) |
| Age 13 | 0.278*** | 0.179*** | 0.391*** | 0.243*** | 0.317*** |
|  | (0.0133) | (0.0110) | (0.0270) | (0.0185) | (0.0193) |
| Age 14 | 0.257*** | 0.167*** | 0.363*** | 0.226*** | 0.292*** |
|  | (0.0147) | (0.0122) | (0.0299) | (0.0202) | (0.0217) |
| Age 15 | 0.211*** | 0.139*** | 0.301*** | 0.194*** | 0.237*** |
|  | (0.0178) | (0.0151) | (0.0359) | (0.0235) | (0.0268) |
| Age 16 | 0.172*** | 0.104*** | 0.275*** | 0.158*** | 0.194*** |
|  | (0.0201) | (0.0184) | (0.0383) | (0.0267) | (0.0302) |
| Age 17 | 0.123*** | 0.0681*** | 0.215*** | 0.114*** | 0.140*** |
|  | (0.0227) | (0.0214) | (0.0436) | (0.0302) | (0.0344) |
| Age 18 | 0.0595** | 0.0303 | 0.114** | 0.0491 | 0.0779** |
|  | (0.0253) | (0.0243) | (0.0490) | (0.0340) | (0.0380) |
| Post-program (after year 2005) | 0.110*** | 0.0630** | 0.184*** | 0.0957** | 0.129*** |
|  | (0.0286) | (0.0279) | (0.0517) | (0.0381) | (0.0438) |
| Post-program* age 6 | 0.143*** | 0.104*** | 0.119** | 0.138*** | 0.150*** |
|  | (0.0282) | (0.0244) | (0.0582) | (0.0363) | (0.0442) |
| Post-program* age 7 | 0.164*** | 0.128*** | 0.126** | 0.167*** | 0.159*** |
|  | (0.0265) | (0.0210) | (0.0569) | (0.0327) | (0.0431) |
| Post-program* age 8 | 0.190*** | 0.135*** | 0.180*** | 0.192*** | 0.185*** |
|  | (0.0248) | (0.0209) | (0.0545) | (0.0301) | (0.0411) |
| Post-program* age 9 | 0.196*** | 0.141*** | 0.191*** | 0.177*** | 0.215*** |
|  | (0.0249) | (0.0208) | (0.0545) | (0.0324) | (0.0389) |
| Post-program* age 10 | 0.182*** | 0.104*** | 0.188*** | 0.157*** | 0.208*** |
|  | (0.0266) | (0.0279) | (0.0553) | (0.0356) | (0.0405) |
| Post-program* age 11 | 0.142*** | 0.0946*** | 0.119** | 0.151*** | 0.130*** |
|  | (0.0305) | (0.0313) | (0.0598) | (0.0377) | (0.0494) |
| Post-program* age 12 | 0.103*** | 0.0962*** | 0.0317 | 0.112*** | 0.0845 |
|  | (0.0333) | (0.0305) | (0.0625) | (0.0421) | (0.0534) |

*(continued next page)*

**Table C.2** *(continued)*

| Variables | (1) All | (2) Urban | (3) Rural | (4) Male | (5) Female |
|---|---|---|---|---|---|
| Post-program* age 13 | 0.0435 (0.0372) | 0.0326 (0.0401) | −0.0173 (0.0636) | 0.0583 (0.0479) | 0.0192 (0.0584) |
| Post-program* age 14 | 0.0634* (0.0365) | 0.0608* (0.0363) | −0.00115 (0.0645) | 0.0604 (0.0481) | 0.0549 (0.0570) |
| Post-program* age 15 | 0.0942*** (0.0347) | 0.0746** (0.0331) | 0.0550 (0.0651) | 0.0839* (0.0463) | 0.0871 (0.0547) |
| Post-program* age 16 | 0.0692* (0.0363) | 0.0657** (0.0332) | 0.00361 (0.0667) | 0.0743 (0.0474) | 0.0422 (0.0576) |
| Post-program* age 17 | 0.0657* (0.0368) | 0.0704** (0.0322) | 0.00293 (0.0684) | 0.0704 (0.0478) | 0.0430 (0.0583) |
| Post-program* age 18 | 0.0445 (0.0381) | 0.0384 (0.0360) | 0.0218 (0.0700) | 0.0393 (0.0506) | 0.0346 (0.0593) |
| Female | −0.0525*** (0.00634) | −0.0395*** (0.00751) | −0.0577*** (0.00914) | | |
| Rural | −0.129*** (0.0106) | | | −0.147*** (0.0137) | −0.0853*** (0.0172) |
| Female-headed household | 0.0384*** (0.00862) | 0.0599*** (0.00981) | 0.0126 (0.0128) | 0.0263** (0.0120) | 0.0447*** (0.0126) |
| Log of per capita consumption | 0.0821*** (0.00444) | 0.0857*** (0.00542) | 0.0698*** (0.00640) | 0.0690*** (0.00604) | 0.0967*** (0.00668) |
| *Mother's education* | | | | | |
| Alphabetization | 0.0517** (0.0248) | −0.0274 (0.0325) | 0.106*** (0.0382) | 0.0731** (0.0320) | 0.0303 (0.0384) |
| EP1 | 0.0801*** (0.0125) | 0.0691*** (0.0106) | 0.0576* (0.0303) | 0.0344* (0.0177) | 0.129*** (0.0178) |
| EP2 | 0.146*** (0.0152) | 0.0755*** (0.0139) | 0.268*** (0.0324) | 0.110*** (0.0210) | 0.189*** (0.0221) |
| ES1 or higher | 0.215*** (0.0204) | 0.129*** (0.0160) | 0.371*** (0.0525) | 0.211*** (0.0250) | 0.227*** (0.0321) |
| Mother absent | −0.0162 (0.0122) | −0.0216 (0.0159) | −0.0160 (0.0164) | −0.00731 (0.0163) | −0.0167 (0.0182) |
| Mother died | −0.0876*** (0.0152) | −0.0850*** (0.0202) | −0.115*** (0.0202) | −0.103*** (0.0221) | −0.0592*** (0.0212) |
| *Father's education* | | | | | |
| Alphabetization | 0.0311 (0.0441) | 0.208*** (0.00586) | −0.179*** (0.0551) | 0.0414 (0.0551) | 0.0567 (0.0695) |
| EP1 | 0.0555*** (0.0116) | 0.0737*** (0.0126) | 0.0267 (0.0170) | 0.0545*** (0.0148) | 0.0612*** (0.0184) |
| EP2 | 0.0791*** (0.0134) | 0.0607*** (0.0123) | 0.131*** (0.0269) | 0.126*** (0.0153) | 0.0103 (0.0233) |
| ES1 or higher | 0.0723*** (0.0200) | 0.0655*** (0.0162) | 0.125** (0.0542) | 0.0828*** (0.0267) | 0.0586* (0.0301) |

*(continued next page)*

**Table C.2** *(continued)*

| Variables | (1)<br>All | (2)<br>Urban | (3)<br>Rural | (4)<br>Male | (5)<br>Female |
|---|---|---|---|---|---|
| Father absent | −0.00590 | 0.0148 | 0.000957 | 0.0118 | −0.0261 |
| | (0.0127) | (0.0161) | (0.0170) | (0.0170) | (0.0189) |
| Father died | −0.00784 | −0.0138 | 0.0166 | 0.0226 | −0.0485** |
| | (0.0121) | (0.0156) | (0.0168) | (0.0154) | (0.0192) |
| District avg travel time to school | −0.000680** | 0.00149*** | −0.00234*** | −0.00107*** | −0.000408 |
| | (0.000264) | (0.000478) | (0.000354) | (0.000355) | (0.000397) |
| District avg consumption (log) | 0.0537*** | 0.0928*** | −0.00573 | 0.00479 | 0.121*** |
| | (0.0108) | (0.0198) | (0.0155) | (0.0143) | (0.0168) |
| Observations | 29,044 | 13,674 | 15,370 | 14,834 | 14,210 |
| Pseudo R-squared | 0.234 | 0.206 | 0.209 | 0.221 | 0.258 |

*Source:* NPS 2008.
*Note:* Provincial dummies were included but not presented here. The referenced categories are no education for mother and father. Standard errors in parentheses.
\*\*\* $p < 0.01$, \*\* $p < 0.05$, \* $p < 0.1$.

that the program has induced many children to attend school earlier, the issue of sending children to school at later ages is not completely resolved. In fact, according to NPS 2008, 76 and 57 percent of non-enrollees ages 6 and 7, respectively, report the main reason for not attending school as "not of school age." In other words, they are still perceived as too young to go to school.

At age 13, the program has insignificant effect, and the size of the coefficient is close to zero, as expected. Surprisingly, the effect starts rising slightly above zero and becomes significant again after the last age of the primary school cycle, around ages 14–16. There are two plausible reasons that explain this rise. First, late entrants are more likely to stay in school during their last few years of primary education. Second, children who started school at the official age and were able to complete primary school are now more likely to attend secondary school. Since education is a sequential process, reducing barriers to obtaining primary education will also produce positive spillover effects on higher education levels. The rise of the effect of the starting age of secondary school following right after a dip at the transitioning age of 13 suggests the presence of a latter effect.

Separate regressions by urban and rural and gender (table C2, columns 2–5) show a similar pattern of the effects of the program over ages, with a larger impact on children ages 6–12 in rural areas and among girls. For older children, the program has a larger effect in urban areas and slightly more for boys, implying that the spillover effects are mainly driven by these sub-samples. Urban children and boys, most of whom have already been in primary schools, now have more opportunity to advance to secondary schools.

## Other Determinants of Enrollment

In all specifications, the effects of other factors are consistent (tables C1 and C2). They show that the demand for schooling in Mozambique shares many characteristics with those of most developing countries. It has a large number of late entrants, strong biases against females (especially in rural areas), lower schooling in rural areas, significant provincial fixed effects, and highly depends on income (with the elasticity higher for girls). Parental education shows the significant and expected positive influence on children's enrollment, while orphans display significant and lower likelihood to be enrolled.

## Notes

1. We observe children up to age 19 for primary school to capture the late entrants and postponed completion due to repetitions and dropouts.
2. Parental education is only available for children younger than age 18 whose parents are at home and alive. In order to make the most use of our sample, we include a variable for parent's missing information and treat missings in parent's education, absence, and death status as zeros (8 percent of mother's information and 19 percent of father's information are missing). We use a similar method for missings in the rural (4.2 percent) and wealth (10 percent) indexes, except that we replace missings with the sample average in the wealth index rather than zeros. District average per capita consumption excludes the specific household consumption. District average travel minutes to school were used because only children who attend school were asked to report time travelling to school.

## References

Duflo, E. 2001. "Schooling and Labor Market Consequences of School Construction in Indonesia: Evidence from an Unusual Policy Experiment." *The American Economic Review* 91 (4): 795–813.

Fox, L., R. M. Benfica, M. Ehrenpreis, M. S. Gaal, H. Nordang, and D. Owen. 2008. *Beating the Odds: Sustaining Inclusion in a Growing Economy: A Mozambique Poverty, Gender, and Social Assessment.* Washington, DC: World Bank.

MEC (Ministério da Educação e Cultura). 2010. "Os resultados do sector através dos principais indicadores." (Progress Report). Ministry of Education and Culture. Government of Mozambique. Maputo, Mozambique.

World Bank. 2005. "Poverty and Social Impact Analysis: Primary School Enrollment and Retention—The Impact of School Fees." World Bank, Washington, DC.

www.ingramcontent.com/pod-product-compliance
Lightning Source LLC
Chambersburg PA
CBHW060342170426
43202CB00014B/2858